Bible-based resources for youth groups

PRESSURE POINTS

Ten issues for 13-18 year olds on
big issues facing young people

Written by Phil Moon and Alan Hewerdine

Edited by Mark Tomlinson

PRESSURE POINTS

WHAT'S IT ALL ABOUT?

There are many issues putting pressure on the lives of young people today. This book deals with just a few of the main ones.

We have tried to give sufficient background material to enable you to tackle each subject with a reasonable degree of confidence, but you will find it helpjul to do some additional reading where possible.

The best single volume covering most of the issues in **Pressure Points** is John Stott's 'Issues Facing Christians Today' (Revised Edition – Marshall Peckering £8.99). We recommend that you obtain a copy for reference and for lending to anyone who wants to go deeper into a particular subject.

The material is deliberately tackled from a Biblical standpoint but does not assume that all group members will be Christians. Some sessions have a clear evangelistic impact.

WHAT'S IN IT?

Notes for youth leaders _____ 3

Session 1
High Society – **Drugs & Alcohol Abuse** _____ 4

Session 2
Boxed In – **Poverty & Homelessness** _____ 10

Session 3
The Grass Is Greener – **Environmental Issues** _____ 16

Session 4
Save Sex – **Sexuality & AIDS** _____ 22

Session 5
Any Dream Won't Do – **Other Faiths** _____ 28

Session 6
Colour Blind – **Racism** _____ 34

Session 7
I Was Hungry And You Held A Concert – **Famine** _____ 40

Session 8
Watch It With Your Eyes Open – **The Media** _____ 46

Session 9
A Twentieth Century God – **Materialism** _____ 52

Session 10
Straight Talk – **Homosexuality** _____ 58

Useful Addresses _____ 64

NOTES FOR YOUTH LEADERS

How you might use this book

Pressure Points can be used in a variety of ways. Each section contains enough material and is set out to provide a programme for a single session. Used in this way, the book as a whole gives a ten week programme.

But we are conscious that all these are big issues and you may want to spend more than one session dealing with them. At the back of the book there is a list of useful addresses of organisations from whom you can get further information and resources to enhance and expand your teaching. Other suggestions are given in the main text.

However, because these are weighty subjects, we would recommend that you do not deal with all ten consecutively without a break to cover something different, unless the group are obviously thriving on the stuff!

You may even choose to use the book to dip into for one-off sessions interspersed with some other series of teaching (like 'All Together Forever' on the book of Ephesians, perhaps!).

Whatever way you choose to use the material, the emphasis of this series is on what the Bible says on these issues. Don't just play the games and ignore what they are trying to teach. Play the games, do the activities, and draw out what the Bible is teaching.

Running Individual Sessions

Each session is laid out in a standard way, with which you will become familiar – there is preparatory material for you as leaders (called *Pre-Match*), followed by the suggested activities themselves. After this comes the *Group Extra* page, which it is worth making good, crisp photocopies of, to give to your group at the right moment in the session.

Here are some hints on running the sessions:

Pray

Teaching young people the Bible is a spiritual activity. Our great desire must be that God will speak to our young people as we teach them the Bible. So pray that he will help you to teach it well, and pray that he will speak to individuals as you do so, and that we will all be obedient listeners. Prayer is the key to effective youth work.

Prepare

Published resources like *Pressure Points* can encourage last minute, rushed and insufficient preparation. You will still need to prepare thoroughly, and well ahead of time. Resist the temptation to let this book do all the work for you. It doesn't! But do read through the session notes two or three weeks beforehand – there are some things which need preparation well ahead.

Select and Adapt

There is no such thing as the ideal resource for your youth group. Whatever resources you use, you will have to select and adapt the material. Select the material you want, because there is far too much for one teaching session, and some of it won't be suitable for your group. Don't take this book to the session – make your own notes of what you will do, and copy them for other leaders if necessary, with approximate timings by the side. And adapt the material which you select, so that it will work in your group.

Variety

As you put together your teaching session, think 'variety'. Use different leaders, if you can. Use different kinds of activities during the session. Use different methods from week to week. Variety is the spice of life.

SESSION 1

High Society – Drugs And Alcohol Abuse

Teaching Point

Christians should look after their bodies by refusing to misuse drugs of any description.

Group Action

Aim that the group will learn to say 'NO' when tempted to get involved with drugs.

Getting Ready

This is a huge topic and to do it justice may require covering the material over two or three sessions. You may like to include some of the activity suggestions on your social programme, such as the **'Coketail Party'** (see *Extra Time*).

You may also find that some of your group have a variety of strongly held opinions on these topics, and probably some members who are involved in some way in the misuse of alcohol, tobacco or other drugs and drug related substances. This will undoubtedly create emotive responses. So know your ground well, and be prepared to talk things through at a more personal level. If you know likely candidates for this in your group, bear this in mind as you prepare.

Throughout this session we will be looking at a number of Bible passages which you will find listed below. Prepare these well and know how they fit into the session.

1 Corinthians 6:19-20 ✓
Proverbs 21:17 ✓
Proverbs 21:1
Isaiah 5:11-12 ✓
Ephesians 5:18 ✓
Proverbs 23:29-35 ✓

Of particular importance is **1 Corinthians 6:19-20**, which Paul originally wrote to the Corinthian Church in the context of sexual immorality, but is applicable in principle to drug/alcohol abuse as it deals with how we treat our bodies.

The passages from **Proverbs, Isaiah and Ephesians** focus on drink and what it does to you. You may not want to use all of these verses so be selective.

Psalm 139, although not directly applicable to drug/alcohol abuse does show that we cannot hide from God and even if we think we can keep our actions secret from Him, He knows all things and sees all things.

Galatians 5:22-23 covers the 'Fruit of the Spirit'. Be sure you highlight '**self control**', and how exercising it will prevent many problems.

Finally **Matthew 6:25-34** and **Romans 14:17-21** focus on the way we live our lives, what we worry about, whether things to do with this life or things of God, and whether we consider the effect our actions have on others.

Equipment

- ✓ Bibles, notebooks, pens, *Group Extra* sheets
- ✓ Paper slips, fireproof bin, matches
- ✓ OHP/screen or posters/roll of paper
- ✓ Marker pens
- ✓ Empty soft drinks cans
- ✓ Artists materials for designing beer cans
- ✓ Materials for custom-made T-shirts
- ✓ Materials for making posters
- ✓ Parents sheets

Music

We Are A Chosen People
Purify My Heart
Shine Jesus Shine
O Lord Your Tenderness
He That Is In Us

Team Talk

There is a wide range of possible activities, don't do them all. Be selective on the basis of your groups ability to handle the subject, but ensure you extract the biblical principles about the way a Christian should live and treat his/her body.

As leader of this session, ensure you maintain a sensitivity to the situation. Meetings like this may strike a raw nerve in some of your young people, and there may be specific areas that will need to be addressed with certain individuals. So be sensitive to these possibilities, as you prepare and during the meeting.

Also, know when you cannot cope with the situation. If it transpires, or you suspect that one of your members is on drugs of some sort, immediately consider who can help you in this. Think about the possibility of informing your minister/elder and/or professional people but do not go off the deep end and involve everyone immediately. Take a carefully considered decision about your course of action.

Finally, as far as is practically possible, keep any discussion groups covering a small age range to ensure each member has a similar level of understanding and experience.

Try one or two of the following, to show how much drugs are a part of our society:

■ 1–SPONSORSHIP

▓ Ask group members to name tobacco and alcohol companies who are involved in the sponsorship of sport and its events.

(The most heavily sponsored sports are Cricket, Formula 1 Motor Racing and Snooker. Others such as Rugby League and Football may have one or two alcohol sponsors but it is unlikely that any would allow tobacco sponsorship).

■ 2–PUB NAMES

▓ Brainstorm the names of local pubs. Prepare yourself to be surprised at how many they know!

■ 3–DRUGS BRAINSTORM

▓ Ask group members to do a cumulative brainstorm. That is they write down two names of drugs, pass the paper to their left, write two more on the one they receive and so on. If at all possible encourage them to avoid repeating ones that have been used already, but they can if they can't think of any new ones.

■ 4–ALCOHOL ADVERTS

▓ Ask group members to cut out adverts for alcohol/cigarettes from a pile of magazines and tape them to another member of the group who becomes a billboard advert. Point out how alcohol/cigarettes are glamourised by the media, and how there is little or no mention of how bad these things are for you.

By explaining to your group that this meeting is about alcohol, smoking and other drugs. Ask them to try and come with an open mind, and simply to see what the Bible is saying on these subjects.

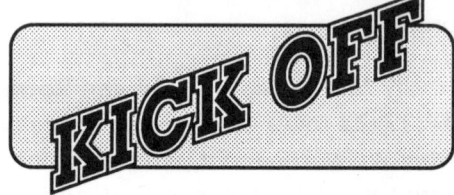

▓ To help this you might like them to write down what they consider to be the three most important things about drugs/alcohol on three separate pieces of paper, then screw these up and put them in the bin. If there is no danger from fire alarms, and it is a metal bin, burn the contents to signify the breaking of their biases.

▓ Then state again that we simply want to see what the Bible is saying on this matter, and be willing for the Bible to shape our thinking, rather than have our thinking shaped by our own prejudices and pre-conceived ideas, and those of our friends, parents and the media.

Begin with one of the following:

■ 1–REASONS ON THE RUN

▓ Organise your group into two or more teams (of two or more people each) and put them on one side of the room. On the other side, each team has a large sheet of paper and a marker pen. On 'Go' the first person runs to the other side of the room and writes on the paper one reason why people drink/take drugs. They run back to their team and the second person does the same etc. No two reasons can be the same. The team with the largest number of different reasons after four minutes is the winner.

■ 2–TRUE/FALSE

■ Ask group members to fill in the *Group Extra* sheet and then discuss it together.

■ Give each member a slip of paper with one of the common drugs written on it, e.g. cannabis, cocaine, crack, heroin, LSD, nicotine, glue, alcohol, barbituates, etc., and put members together in groups according to these drugs. In these groups they should study the six Bible passages in *Getting Ready* and use them to answer the question: **'What's wrong with drugs?'**. Put the question up on the Overhead Projector or on posters around the room.

■ You may need to remind your group that modern day drugs and tobacco weren't known then – so aren't mentioned by name in the Bible. So look for principles which are relevant to the use and misuse of drugs and alcohol today.

■ Collate the answers on an overhead projector/poster. Top up and comment as appropriate. Drum home the main point from **1 Corinthians 6:19 & 20** that God wants us to look after our bodies. Drug misuse abuses our body.

■ If you have time, read **Psalm 139:1-18** and explain that you can't 'Get away' with drug misuse thinking that God won't notice. Nothing is a secret to Him.

In groups of three or four, give each group a drink can, and ask them to cover the can with paper and design a new 'Can of Beer' with a Biblical health warning about the dangers of excessive drinking.

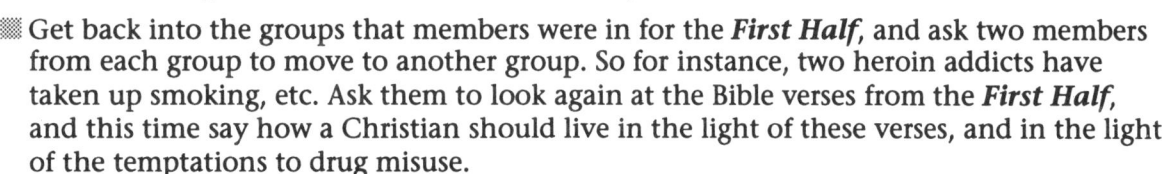

Kick off this session by asking your group members to summarize the *First Half* by completing the following:

■ 'If I asked God what His attitude toward drinking and drugs was, I think He'd say ....' Put this on the OHP or a poster, so that members can easily see it.

■ Get back into the groups that members were in for the *First Half*, and ask two members from each group to move to another group. So for instance, two heroin addicts have taken up smoking, etc. Ask them to look again at the Bible verses from the *First Half*, and this time say how a Christian should live in the light of these verses, and in the light of the temptations to drug misuse.

■ Introduce them to **Romans 14:17-21**, **Galatians 5:22** (especially the self control), again asking how Christians should live in the light of these verses.

■ Ask your group what **Matthew 6:25-34** has to do with drug misuse. Explain that it is saying that the antidote to worrying about the things of this world is to be concerned about the things of God.

■ If you have time, as a separate project, ask members to think up slogans for anti drink/drugs T-shirts. For example, 'No Thanks' or 'Just Say No' or 'Alive - Naturally' may get your members thinking, and then ask them to make their own T-shirts with these slogans and T-shirt paint. If you buy in a stock of large plain white T-shirts and paint, this could be a good part of an evening on this subject.

Most of the meeting has focussed on explaining why you shouldn't get involved in alcohol/drug abuse, but there may be members in your group who already have.

- Take this opportunity to explain sensitively that our human nature is such that we do fail God and make mistakes but that He does give us hope IN Christ, by being prepared to forgive us of anything provided we are truly sorry. He is the only one who is able to give us a *New Start*. This is what is meant by God's GRACE, an undeserved free gift.

- If your group are artistic, ask them to make posters on the theme 'Enjoy God Not Drugs', and then decorate your meeting room with these for the coming few weeks. But don't keep them up for too long and let them get tatty, and let your group know now that they will only be up for a limited amount of time.

- It would be good to close the evening quietly, by praying together for the members' personal response to this session. Pray too for those who are abusing drugs of all sorts, for those who legislate about advertising, for those who help the drug abusers, for parents and children of drug abusers, etc. Maybe ask the members to pray silently as you lead them.

▩ COKETAIL PARTY

- Try this, either as part of your teaching evening, or as a full blown party in its own right. Get recipes for Coketails from the Band of Hope (see Address List on page 64) or try some of the following:

- These are three cheap Coketails:

    - **Shirley Temple:** Mix together in a glass of Ginger Beer, A dash of Grenadine Syrup, a slice of lemon, a cherry, ice and a straw and parasol.

    - **Cherry Bite:** Mix together ice, ⅓ cherry nectar, ⅔ dry ginger, a dash of lime, a lemon slice and a straw.

    - **Miss Fizz:** Mix together ice, ½ glass of Passion Fruit nectar, a dash of lime cordial, top up with soda water, add a slice of orange/cherry, straw and a stirrer.

▩ ALCOHOLICS ANONYMOUS

- Ask a speaker from this organisation to come and tell your group their story. Alcoholics Anonymous is not a specifically Christian organisation, but this can be a real eye opener to the dangers of alcohol abuse.

▩ PARENTS SHEETS

- Some groups use 'Parents' Sheets' for subjects like this. This is an attractive sheet of discussion questions which group members discuss with their parents. Make them look attractive, and for this particular subject, include questions like:

    'Why do adults drink?'

    'Why do teenagers drink?'

    'Should cannabis be legalised?' 'Why?'

    'Why do people start taking drugs?', etc.

    (Use this idea carefully depending on the type of group you have)

GROUP EXTRA

TRUE OR FALSE

STATEMENT	TRUE	FALSE
Drinking keeps me alert		
I can sleep it off		
Drinking warms me up		
Soft drugs never did anyone any harm		
Alcoholics are born not made		
Cannabis turns you on		
Alcohol is a depressant		
Nicotine is one of the most addictive drugs in the world		
Light beers will never get you drunk		
If you know your limits you'll never get caught drink-driving		
I can give up at any time I want		

SESSION 2

Boxed In – Poverty And Homelessness

Teaching Point

That God cares deeply about the poor and expects us to act on their behalf.

Group Action

That the group should re-think their own lifestyle in the light of the poverty of others and should act against injustice which makes and keeps the poor, poor.

Getting Ready

This session will deal with three issues.
1) How do we define poverty?
2) What is God's attitude towards poverty and those who are poor?
3) What should we do about poverty?

As with several other subjects dealt with in this book, it is an issue which, if treated seriously, will make us think deeply, feel uncomfortable and ought to lead to radical action.

There is a great temptation to water down, re-interpret or explain away much of what we find difficult, in order to justify our own lifestyle. If we are to teach this subject with integrity, we need to beware of being seen to present a 'do as I say and not as I do' image. Tackling issues with young people without a willingness to face up to it honestly on a personal level may result in cynicism on their part. This could well affect their whole attitude to the Bible and the Christian Faith.

On the other hand, if we and our group members were to act upon the teaching in this section, the impact for good could be far reaching.

1) God's attitude to the poor

Proverbs 14:31 & 19:17 express the positive and negative ways in which God identifies personally with the poor. **Psalm 10** starts with a cry of anguish at God's apparent lack of concern but **v.14 & 17-18** assert that God is indeed deeply concerned about those who are oppressed. **James 2:1-7** warns against discriminating against the poor and shows God's positive attitude towards them in spiritual terms. **2 Corinthians 8:9** reveals the extent to which God went to identify with the poor. Jesus became poor so that we might become rich. Whilst our 'riches' are to be understood in a spiritual sense, His poverty was material.

2) God's action on behalf of the poor

Deuteronomy 26:5-10 reminds the Israelites of how God had taken them from poverty and oppression and brought them into great material blessing. **Psalm 146** is a celebration in song of God's action on behalf of a whole range of poor and oppressed people. In **Luke 1:46-55**, Mary echoes these same thoughts and in **Luke 4:18-19** Jesus quotes **Isaiah 61:1-2** as setting out the terms of reference for His ministry, which is primarily concerned with the poor and other victims of deprivation.

3) God's attitude to the rich

Luke 12:13-21 warns against material greed and wealth as hindrances to spiritual prosperity. **Luke 18:18-25** makes a similar point. In **Luke 16:19-31**, the rich man is condemned for failing to help the poor beggar. **James 2:1-7** warns about showing favouritism towards the rich who are often responsible for exploiting the poor.

4) God's action against the rich

Amos 5:11-16 & 6:1-7 presents God's impending action against those who exploit the poor and the idle rich who do nothing to help them. **Isaiah 10:1-4** gives a similar warning. Both prophecies were fulfilled in the destruction and exile of Israel and Judah. **Luke 1:46-55** speaks of God's action in humbling the powerful and sending the rich away empty. **James 5:1-5** is an uncompromising condemnation of rich people who exploit and neglect the poor.

Equipment

- ✓ At least 1 week before – *Group Extra* sheets for survey
- ✓ Bibles, notebooks, pens
- ✓ *Poverty in Britain* Statistics photocopy/on acetate.
- ✓ Survey results photocopy/on acetate
- ✓ OHP/screen or posters/roll of paper
- ✓ *World Incomes* figures photocopy/on acetate.
- ✓ OHP pens/acetate or marker pens
- ✓ Group Bible Study sheets with relevant passages listed.
- ✓ Equipment for 'Hard Sell' game (See *Half Time*).
- ✓ Addresses for further information

Music

Lord We Long For You (Heal Our Nation)

O Lord The Clouds Are Gathering

You Laid Aside Your Majesty

Soften My Heart

Team Talk

This is a big subject and you will probably need more than one session to do it justice. You may want to divide the material in such a way as to cover the personal, church and social aspects separately. If you choose to do so, we recommend that you incorporate some element of practical response in each session rather than dealing with all the 'theory' and then the practical.

At least a week beforehand use the *Group Extra* sheets to carry out an anonymous survey within the group.

- Analyze the information and publish the results on photocopied sheets/O.H.P. during **Warm Up**. Aim to identify:

    Highest/Average/Lowest income and expenditure.

- You may wish to extend the exercise by getting the group to carry out the survey amongst school friends. A few of them with access to computers may be willing and able to prepare the results for you.

Ask each member to look at the survey results and decide whether they would describe themselves as rich, poor or average in relation to the rest of the group? Get them to move to designated areas of the room labelled 'rich', 'poor' and 'average'.

What do we mean by poor? In the exercise above we assessed our own 'wealth' or 'poverty' in comparison to our immediate social group. Is this a true measure? What happens if we compare ourselves with other groups?

- Display the following statistics and statements on poverty in Britain:

    - In 1989, 12 million had incomes less than half the national average. (The E.C. definition of poverty).
    - 1/2 million are officially homeless.
    - Over 1 million homes are considered unfit for human habitation.
    - 10 million cannot afford adequate housing.
    - 7 million go without essential clothing.
    - 5 million cannot afford to eat properly.
    - 6.5 million cannot afford one or more essential household items like carpets or a fridge.

    (Sources: 'Breadline Britain 1990's' and a Government report 'Households Below Average Income'.)

- Ask the group to think again whether they are rich, poor or average in comparison with the rest of Britain. Then reveal these other statistics on the U.K. from the same government report:

    - amongst the poorest 10 per cent of the population, the proportion in possession of a telephone rose from 50 per cent in 1979 to 70 per cent in 1989.
    - of the bottom 10 per cent of the population in 1989, 50 per cent were in households with a video, compared with 60 per cent of the total population.

- Follow them with the figures in Table 1. on world income levels for 1989:

TABLE 1 – AVERAGE ANNUAL INCOME PER HEAD OF POPULATION (This is just a small sample.)

Mozambique	£53	Zambia	£256	United Kingdom	£9,612
Ethiopia	£79	Bolivia	£407	U.S.A.	£13,757
Somalia	£112	Zimbabwe	£428	Norway	£14,664
Bangladesh	£118	Philippines	£467	Japan	£15,664
India	£224	Honduras	£592	Switzerland	£19,658

- Ask the group for a third time to decide whether they are rich, poor or average, when compared to the rest of the world.

- Split into four groups. Give each group the Bible references on one of the sections outlined in *Getting Ready* and ask them to answer the relevant question below:

    1) How does God feel about the poor?
    2) What does/will God do for the poor?
    3) How does God feel about the rich?
    4) What does/will God do to the rich?

Play 'Hard Sell'.
(Reproduced with permission from TEAR Fund).

- You need: 60 large beans, 4 small bowls, 4 pens, paper, 20 coins (1p).

- Preparation: Divide into four groups. Three are producer countries trying to sell beans. The fourth is a buyer. Put one group in each corner of the room. Give each 'producer' 10 beans in a bowl, and a pen and paper. Give the 'buyer' the coins in a bowl.

- Object of the game: The 'producers' aim to sell beans *for as much as possible*. After four rounds a 'producer' with 2p will starve; 5p will be hungry; anything more will be O.K.

- The 'buyer' aims to buy 10-15 beans *as cheaply as possible*. If he pays more than 1p a bean he makes a loss. If he gets less than 10 beans he goes broke. He doesn't need more than 15.

- Procedure:
    1) Explain the game. Emphasize the underlined bits.
    2) Each 'producer' makes a written offer (e.g. 3 beans for 2p). These offers are collected by the referee and taken to the 'buyer'.
    3) The 'buyer' decides which offers to take up and which to reject.
    4) Any accepted 'producer' is called over and the exchange is made. The 'buyer' can write a note on the other papers which are then returned.
    5) Repeat steps (2)–(4) up to three times, i.e. four rounds in all.

- Feedback: Is the game fair? Which is worse, starving or going broke? Who controls the price? What would happen if the 'producers' got together to fix a price?

The game shows how a system of trading can be weighted in a way which favours the rich 'buyer' countries against the poor 'producer' nations. This is the world we live in.

- Now present the following situation:

    'A farmer's crops fail and he has to sell his land to buy food for his family. But he has now lost his source of income.'

- How would you prevent this family from remaining poor? Brainstorm ideas in small groups.

- Compare with **Leviticus 25**. By question and answer, identify and list (on paper/O.H.P.) the following rules:

    1) NO DEBT TRAP (**V.13**) – land to be returned.
    2) NO EXPLOITATION (**V.14-17**) – land values to be based on the number of years to the next Jubilee.
    3) INCENTIVES TO WORK (**V.25-28**) – the seller retained the right to buy the land back once he acquired the means to do so.
    4) EARNING CAPACITY SECURED (**V.29-31**) – homes in rural areas were tied to the land and thus the means of livelihood. They were to be returned at the Jubilee.

5) **NO LOAN SHARKS (V.35-38)** – money borrowed because of poverty was not liable to interest.
6) **NO BURDEN ON SUCCESSIVE GENERATIONS (V.39-43 & 47-55)** – an Israelite and *his family* would be released at the Jubilee.

▪ Sadly there is no reference in the Old Testament to indicate that the law of Jubilee was ever implemented. The early Church, as a society in a society, clearly set out to model the Jubilee principles in their life together. Discuss with the group the parallels between the provisions of the Jubilee Year and the lifestyle of the early Church as set out in **Acts 2:41-47; 4:32-37; 2 Corinthians 8:13-15**.

Discuss practical ways in which your group can respond realistically to what they have discovered. Aim to do so, however, on each of these levels:

1) Personal lifestyle. Discuss this quotation:
'The rich must live more simply that the poor may simply live.'
(Dr. Charles Birch in a plenary address to the World Council of Churches Fifth Assembly 1st Dec.1975)

▪ How can I live more simply?

2) Church lifestyle.
'Somehow the pressures of modern society were making it increasingly difficult for us to live by the values we had been taught. We thought our church should constitute a community of believers capable of withstanding these pressures, yet it seemed to go along with things as they were instead of encouraging an alternative. The 'pillars' of the church seemed as severely trapped by material concerns and alienation as most non-christians we knew.'
(Dave & Neta Jackson, 'Living Together In A World Falling Apart', Creation House, 1974)

▪ Does this describe my church? If so, what can I do to influence my church for change?

3) Social Structures. Consider this quotation:
'The present social order is the most abject failure the world has ever seen....Governments have never learned yet how to distribute the fruits of the industry of their people. The countries of the earth produce enough to support all, and if the earnings of each was fairly distributed it would make all men toil some, but no man toil too much. This great civilization of ours has not learned so to distribute the produce of human toil so that it shall be equitably held. Therefore the government breaks down.'
(C.I. Scofield, author of the Scofield Bible Notes, 1903)

▪ Have things changed for the better since 1903? How can we influence governments to change social structures in favour of the poor?

▪ Make a note of suggestions made and follow through on them. Plan a later session to review how far they have been implemented.

1. Discuss with the group to what extent they think the credibility of Jesus' mission, as stated in **Luke 4:16-21**, was affected by his lifestyle and that of his disciples. (See **Luke 9:57-62; 10:1-9; 18:18-30**.) What does this say to us about our mission today?

2. How seriously can we take Jesus' words in **Matthew 6:19-34**? John Wesley said that Christians should give away all but 'the plain necessaries of life' – that is plain, wholesome food, clean clothes and enough to carry on one's business. One should earn what one can, justly and honestly. But all income should be given to the poor after one satisfies bare necessities. ('The Works of John Wesley', London: Wesleyan Conference Office, 1872) Wesley lived what he preached. Sales of his books often earned him £1,400 annually, but he spent only £28 on himself.

3. For additional ideas TEAR Fund's magazine '3rd Track' is well worth subscribing to.

GROUP EXTRA

MY INCOME

SOURCE	AMOUNT Per wk/mth*
Pocket money	....
Clothing allowance	....
Dinner money	....
Bus (or other) fares	....
Part-time job	....
Other earings (eg. for doing household chores)	....
TOTAL (A)	....

MY EXPENSES

COMMITMENT	AMOUNT Per wk/mth*
Food	....
Clothing	....
Travel	....
Other (1)	....
Other (2)	....
Other (3)	....
TOTAL (B)	....

My disposable income, to spend as I choose, is:

TOTAL (A) – TOTAL (B) ....

*Decide before filling in the sheet whether figures will be given per week or per month and be consistent. If income and expenses are not given on the same basis you will need to make an adjustment before working out disposable income.

SESSION 3

The Grass Is Greener – The Environment

Teaching Point

God has made us his estate manager's on earth and therefore we should look after the earth responsibly.

Group Action

Aim that the group would put into practice some practical and specific response to the commands to look after the environment responsibly.

Getting Ready

Leaders have a responsibility to teach what the Bible is saying and not what we and/or our young people think it's saying. So all the time try to help your young people get away from what they already think and see what the Bible is saying. This is often a long term process, as we try to get our young people to submit to the Bible. Attitudes and preconceptions often change gradually, but it's worth your effort.

Sustained practical action will probably need to be maintained by the leaders, so be sure you are enthusiastic enough to carry this on. Good resolutions unfulfilled can be very damaging.

The Fall
In **Genesis 3:14-19** we are able to see some of the changes to God's handiwork that were brought about through the 'Fall'.

Below is a list of some of the changes that were for the worse and spoilt what was good.

- the animal kingdom (**v 14**)
- interaction between animals and human beings (**v 15**)
- procreation (**v 16**)
- relationships between people, especially men and women (**v 16**)
- the ground (**v 17**)
- the plant kingdom (**v 18**)
- work becomes toil (**v 19**)
- death is introduced (**v 19**)

Equipment

✓ Bibles, notebooks, pens, *Group Extra* sheets
✓ OHP/screen/sheet paper and marker pens
✓ Slide projector/camera and film or TV/VCR and camcorder
✓ Selection of newspapers/magazines, backing paper, glue and scissors

Music

The Earth Is The Lord's (And Everything In It)
O Lord My God (How Great Thou Art)
O Lord Our God How Majestic Is Your Name
Jesus Is Lord, Creation's Voice Proclaims It
Ah, Lord God
Lord Of Lord's, King Of King's

Team Talk

The knee-jerk Christian response to green issues is to say that we must look after the earth, and so we thoughtlessly begin to treat the earth as if it were some sort of god.

In this session we aim to teach members to think Biblically about our responsibilities to the created world which God has set us over.

First Half establishes God's ideal for the care of the environment and points to the responsibility God has given to us to rule over his world.

Second Half explains the impact that the Fall has had on this and shows some of the results in the exploitation of the environment by us.

And then *Final Whistle* points out some of the implications for us now. Help your members think these through, and try to avoid the thoughtless and careless 'save the planet' response. You may end up at this point, but make sure your members realise why they believe this is the correct response, if they do.

Begin by drawing your members attention to the impact man has had on the environment. You could do this in any one of a number of ways:

■ 1 BLACK-OUT

■ Turn out the lights and turn on the OHP. Obtain facts and figures from some of the addresses listed on page 64 and tell your members the impact people have had on the environment.

■ As you do so, put headline style acetates on the OHP, or gradually cover up the OHP with card until it is completely covered.

■ If you don't have an OHP you could start with a darkened room and put environmental facts up on the wall, illuminating each with a torch, or illuminate them all and then turn the torches off in turn after each point is stated, ending in darkness.

■ 2 BARN-STORM

■ Ask your group to barnstorm (yes, barnstorm) onto the OHP/sheet of paper some of the environmental changes people have made to the world. Ask your group which are good and which are bad, and make sure they say why they believe these are good and bad changes. You could have an outline picture of a barn on to which you brainstorm changes, in order to make a change from the usual plain blank sheet of paper.

■ 3 SLIDES

■ In the weeks before the meeting, arrange for members of your group to help you take some slides of your local area, showing how people have affected the environment. Main roads/factories/quarries are obvious examples. What about housing estates, canals, railways, farming (almost all of England/Wales used to be oak forest many years ago, and would be still were it not for farming). Develop the slides and show them at the meeting. Ask your group which of the slides they consider to show an acceptable picture and why?

■ Using a video camera is slightly easier – you don't have to wait for processing. Some church members may have a video camcorder which you may be able to borrow for the meeting.

Summarise your groups findings from the *Warm Up* and outline the main content of the session:

'that God has made us his estate manager's on earth, and we should therefore look after it responsibly.'

■ Ask members to clear their minds of ideas they may already hold on this subject, and be ready to learn, accept and obey what the Bible has to say.

■ To possibly help achieve an open mind on this subject you may like them to write what they think about the environment on a scrap of paper, and to then fold this up and put it in a bin. Now pray that we would all be open to learn God's mind on the environment.

Ask your members to look up **Genesis 1:26-28**, **Genesis 2:15** and **Psalm 8:6-8**, or display these passages on the OHP or on three large cards on the wall.

18

- Divide into threes, and give each group a slip of paper with the following words on:

> - **A–** "These verses mean that we have complete control over the earth and can do what we like with it. We are told to 'fill the earth and subdue it' (**Genesis 1:28**). We can exploit the environment because God has handed control of the planet over to us, no strings attached. Environmental issues aren't really important for the Christian."
> - **B–** "We are told to take care of the earth, so we should look after it as if it were our own. This must be a high priority for the Christian, and should affect our thinking and living at every point. Recycling, and all other forms of environmental care are essential for the Christian."
> - **C–** "We are made in the image of God, and this involves ruling over the earth as God's representatives. Because we are in the image of God, we should rule the earth as God would, responsibly, justly, and sensibly. Dominion is not the same as exploitation. Neither is it to treating the earth as 'god'. We should look after it carefully and responsibly."

- Ask your groups to choose the statement which best reflects the belief they hold on the basis that none of the wording may be changed. (If time allows, you may want them to amend the statement to reflect what they believe more closely).
- This resource is written in the belief that (**C**) is the only Biblical position, and as you guide the teaching, you may like to ensure that this is understood by your group.

JOB DESCRIPTION

- Ask your members to write a job description for the caretaker of Planet earth. Work in teams of two or three, with these headings:

    1- Job title   2- Responsible for   3- Responsible to   4- Hours of work   5- Main tasks
    6- Equipment provided   7- Disciplinary procedure (result of failure or inefficiency)

Try one or more of these:

1 – Environmental Awareness
Discuss with your group what you could do to help your church to be more environmentally aware. You could introduce the idea here and get them to jot down some ideas and then take it up again at the end once you've covered the session material properly.

2 – Recycling Project
Discuss the possibility of running a church bottle bank or other recycling project. Make sure if you are going to do this, that its a long term commitment and not just a flash in the pan. Put off the final decision until next week or the week after, and don't be swayed by initial enthusiasm which may wane with time.

3 – What a State!
As an introduction to *Second Half*, discuss with your group how they feel about the state of the world and why they feel that way.

4 – The World and Me
If your group don't share their feelings well, use 'The World and Me' sheet from *Group Extra*, and ask them to use it to help them express their feelings about the state of the world. Use this as a basis and springboard for discussion.

SECOND HALF

First Half has established God's ideal for the care of the environment, and this is what questions should be aiming at.

- In *Second Half* you will need to show your group what affect the Fall has had on our management of the environment, and then begin to work through (in this section and in *Final Whistle*) how they can apply what they have learned, and turn theory into action.

- Ask your members to look at **Genesis 3:14-19**, and with this as a base to brainstorm onto the OHP/large sheet of paper some of the effects of the Fall. Or you could give a short input, outlining the impact of the Fall and covering the points set out in *Getting Ready*.

- You will need to explain that the Fall affects the environment directly, and indirectly through our actions and attitudes. Ask group members to brainstorm some of our sins (e.g. selfishness, pride, etc.) onto the left hand side of a piece of paper, and then write down the impact this has on the environment on the right hand side.

FINAL WHISTLE

This section is important as it points to practical action that can be taken.

- Ask members, in groups of three to complete the 'A world of difference' sheet on the *Group Extra* page. Try being 'Devils advocate' – some of the statements are deliberately provocative.

- Remind members especially of the teaching in the *First Half* about people ruling the world, and being called to rule the way God does – carefully and responsibly. Avoid some of the more extreme responses of environmentalism, and aim for an action plan for individual and or group action to be taken.

EXTRA TIME

Try some of the following:

- **1** – Try this tension getter in the *Second Half* or *Final Whistle*. "Belinda is a good friend of yours, but recently she's gone Green. She recycles everything, won't use any cosmetics that are tested on animals, has become a vegan, has thrown away all her mum's non-ozone aerosols, cycles to school refusing to go in the school bus because of the pollution it causes, and is supporting 'Save the Whale' and 'Save the Mother Earth' badges, as well as a Greenpeace T-shirt. She criticises you for going on holiday to a country with high pollution levels, and for using a supermarket where the carrier bags don't biodegrade, and claims that everyone should live like she does."

    What do you say?   Why?

    Is Belinda being sensible?   Are you being half-hearted?

- **2** – Give members a selection of newspapers and magazines and ask them to cut out articles or headlines from these in order to create an environment collage, highlighting the impact we have had on this world. Use this collage in the *Warm Up* section.

- **3** – Hold a Court Case for *Half Time*, as a follow on from *First Half*. One group member is accused of not looking after the planet responsibly. Have a defendant, witnesses, a leader as judge, and a prosecutor and defence council, both with assistants. This will take some preparation to set up but will be fun and instructive. Give each person a careful brief of what the defendant has/has not done. Other group members form the jury.

GROUP EXTRA

THE WORLD AND ME

How do you feel about the following?
(Pick one or more of the suggested words which reflect your feelings)

* "100 square mile oil slick which destroys arctic shoreline"
* "Children dying of lead poisoning from car exhausts"
* "Osprey stops breeding in Britain"
* "Greenbelt being eaten up"
* "Famine hits Africa again as rains fail"
* "Storms wreck Russian wheat harvest"
* " Acid rain destroying cathedral"
* "Global warming will melt ice caps"
* "Town decides against another recycling point"
* "Some whale species facing possible extinction"

Amazed	Hilarious	Relieved
Amused	Hot and bothered	Resentful
Angry	Jealous	Sick
Annoyed	Joyful	Surprised
Anxious	Not bothered	Tearful
Bitter	Perplexed	Unfair
Despairing	Pleased	Upset
Don't care	Puzzled	Up tight
Enraged	Relaxed	Worried

A WORLD OF DIFFERENCE

ACTIVITY	RIGHT or WRONG?	WHY?
Coal mining (pit)		
Open-cast coal mining		
Open-cast coal mining in Siberia		
Letting the Do-Do die out		
Dropping litter		
Using unrecycled paper		
Using coloured loo paper		
Eating dolphin-hazardous tuna		
Eating tuna		
Depleting fish stocks in the North Sea		
Reading a newspaper		
Using leaded petrol		
Forgetting to use the bottle bank		
Burning logs in a smokeless zone		
Using aerosol deodorant		

SESSION 4

Save Sex – Sexuality And A.I.D.S.

Teaching Point

Sex is a gift from God that is good and can only be fully enjoyed within a faithful marriage relationship.

Group Action

Aim that the group will feel positively about their own sexuality and accept God's Biblical guidelines as the best for their lives and the only truly 'safe sex'.

Getting Ready

The Church has for the most part failed young people in the area of teaching on sexuality, largely through its embarrassed silence. This has conveyed one of three messages:

a) sex is a taboo subject for Christians, because it is somehow wrong, dirty, or, at best, slightly distasteful;

b) sex is enjoyable; God is anti-sex and, therefore, anti-enjoyment;

c) the Bible has nothing relevant to say on the subject.

As a result of these negative messages, young people have gained a distorted view of their own sexuality and sexual behaviour. The aim of this session is to present the Biblical teaching on sexuality as positive not negative.

It is a subject which needs to be handled with care and sensitivity, having regard to potentially wide variations in sexual development and awareness in the group, even for young people of similar age.

God's foundation for Sexual Relationships:

Genesis 1:28 contains the first recorded words spoken to people and they are about sex! God's first command was to reproduce.

Genesis 2:23 contains the first recorded words spoken by people and they are about sexuality! Adam recognised in Eve the only being who could fully complement himself, because she shared his human nature but was sexually different.

And **Genesis 2:24** records the result of God's creation of sexuality and people's recognition of it – the leaving of the parent-child relationship, the joining together of man and woman in the marriage relationship and their complete physical union in a sexual relationship.

Equipment

- ✓ Bibles, notebooks, pens, *Group Extra* sheets
- ✓ OHP/screen or posters/roll of paper
- ✓ OHP pens/acetate or marker pens
- ✓ Paper, pens/pencils for 'Consequences'.
- ✓ Top Twenty singles photocopied or on acetate
- ✓ Video clips/magazine extracts of adverts.
- ✓ Sample letters from Problem Page of teen magazines.

Music

In My Life Lord, Be Glorified
Jesus You Are Changing Me
O Lord Your Tenderness
He Walked Where I Walk

Team Talk

It is statistically probable that there will be some young people within your group who are already sexually active. It is important to present these issues in a way which is not condemning, but may lead on to the need for repentance, forgiveness and a change of lifestyle. Jesus did not condemn the woman caught in adultery but he did say 'Go and sin no more.'

Be prepared for follow-up counselling where necessary. This should be done confidentially with members of the *same* sex, so leaders who are normally solo will need to get someone else in.

It will probably be useful to have available copies of Christian books on the subject. For suggestions, contact 'Christian Initiative on Teenage Sexuality' (See Address List on page 64).

Parents need to be informed that you will be dealing with these issues, as they may view such teaching as their responsibility not yours. Write to them and encourage them to contact you with their comments.

Play the game of 'Consequences'.

- Each person is given a sheet of paper and the following verbal instructions:

    1). At the top, write an adjective describing a boy, e.g. handsome, shy, talkative, etc.

    2). Fold paper over to cover the word written and pass to the person on your right.

    3). Add a boy's name to the paper, fold it over and pass on as before.

    4). Continue by adding the following: adjective describing a girl, girl's name, where they met, when they met, what he said to her, what she said to him, the 'consequence'. Each time the paper is folded over before passing it on.

    5). Unfold the papers and read out in turn.

- With a large group, you may need to split into smaller groups to speed up the exercise or only read out a small sample of the more amusing stories.

By pointing out that even the briefest of relationships can have consequences which we haven't thought about. Despite the large volume of media attention given to 'love' and 'sex', it is still an area in which people have a lot of problems and questions.

Try this:

- **1)** Give each person a sheet or display on O.H.P. a list of the current (or recent) Top Twenty singles. Ask them to identify how many of them are 'love' songs or those which deal in some way with male/female relationships.

- **2)** Show a few video clips or distribute extracts from magazines of adverts which in some way use sexual images to promote the product. (Avoid the more lurid variety.)

- **3)** Get volunteers to read sample letters from the 'Problem Page' of teen magazines. Try to include a balance of letters from both sexes. (Again avoid being too 'sensational', the aim is to demonstrate the larger number of letters on sex related issues.)

- We can draw the following conclusions from these sources of information:

    1) Sex and sexuality are major topics of interest.

    2) Sexual images have a powerful influence on us (especially, it seems, our buying habits).

    3) Sexuality and sexual behaviour are also major causes of personal problems.

- If these conclusions are correct, then it would be surprising if God did not have quite a lot to say on the subject.

- Using the outline in *Getting Ready* on **Genesis 1:28** & **2:23** show how right from the beginning, God was concerned to lay a proper foundation for our sexual relationships. God is not anti-sex – He invented it!

Prepare in advance several 'Consequences' stories along the lines of the game but with less humorous tales to tell.

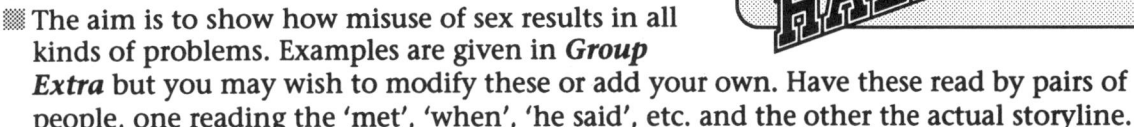

- The aim is to show how misuse of sex results in all kinds of problems. Examples are given in *Group Extra* but you may wish to modify these or add your own. Have these read by pairs of people, one reading the 'met', 'when', 'he said', etc. and the other the actual storyline.

Since the Sixties, the popular image of sex and sexuality is very idealised with little reference to any negative consequences. The 'pill', abortion and liberalised social attitudes, all encourage young people to see sex as fun, attractive, normal and safe, without any commitment to marriage. All that has been radically altered by the impact of A.I.D.S.

- There have always been negative consequences to sex outside marriage, but in the past few decades we have managed to find some way to get round them. If contraception failed, there was abortion or support could be provided for the single parent. Some sexually transmitted diseases (STD's), once fatal like A.I.D.S., became treatable. It seems there's always a way to carry on with unrestricted, consequence-free sex, so with A.I.D.S. it is surely only a matter of time. In the meantime we will just have to put up with the inconvenience of practising 'safe sex'.

- What is the Christian response? Point out to the group the failure of the so-called solutions offered by contraception, abortion, etc. It was argued that the pill would reduce unwanted pregnancies, in fact they have gone up. Legalising abortion was supposed to put an end to back-street abortions, but these too have increased. If the number of new cases of STD's were cases of 'flu, or measles, we would call it an epidemic. Statistical information can be obtained from sources in the Address List on page 64.

- A.I.D.S. is undoubtedly frightening some people into rethinking their sexual behaviour, but the major emphasis is on a) finding a cure, and b) minimising the risk in the meanwhile, not on how and when our sexuality should find its proper expression.

- The success or failure of the medical profession to provide for risk-free sex overlooks a more fundamental issue, that of relationships. The Bible's message about sex is overwhelmingly concerned with presenting marriage as the God-given pattern for a relationship which is secure, permanent and exclusive and which provides, therefore, the setting within which the intimacy of sex can best be enjoyed. Anything else is second best or worse.

- Read and discuss **2 Samuel 13:1-19** with the group. How genuine do they think Amnon's love for Tamar was? What was he seeking from the relationship? How did it change when he got what he wanted? What were Tamar's feelings both before and after she was raped? Discuss the relevance of this story in today's world. You may want to refer to cases of so-called 'date rape'.

- Handle this with extreme care. There may be those who have suffered rape or sexual abuse in your group.

- God's laws limiting sex to within marriage are not negative prohibitions aimed at reducing the enjoyment of sex, but positive safeguards designed to protect a precious gift from being spoiled and devalued.

- Of course, simply being married does not automatically guarantee a wonderful sex-life, but it does provide the right context in which to learn how to properly express our God-created sexuality. That is why God also gives clear instruction about rights and responsibilities within marriage in order that the relationship does provide the love and security it is intended to.

- Display on O.H.P. or a poster the words: MOSES SAID.... Get someone to read **Genesis 2:24**. Uncover a further section of the acetate/poster saying: JESUS SAID.... Get someone to read **Matthew 19:5**. Uncover the third section which reads: PAUL SAID.... Get someone to read **Ephesians 5:31**. All three quotations are the same. Add an overlay or uncover a final section with the quotation written out. This could be used as a memory verse.

- Walter Trobisch in his book, 'I Married You', equates leaving of parents with the legal, public aspect of marriage, being united with the more personal aspect of a loving commitment to one another, and becoming one flesh with the intimacy of sexual intercourse. All three aspects – the outward, practical, social aspect; the deep emotional and personal aspect; and the intimate physical one – are necessary to provide wholeness to the relationship.

- Draw a triangle on acetate or paper and label the corners – marriage, love, sex. Removal of any one corner leaves an incomplete, 2-dimensional relationship.

Discuss with the group how a truly Biblical, positive view of both sex and marriage compares with current social attitudes and the message of 'safe sex'.

- Celibacy outside and faithfulness inside marriage are not the norm. Our young people need to take to themselves these standards as an expression of God's love not a restriction of their freedom. As in all other areas of life, we need God's help if we are to live out his plans for our lives. Conclude with a prayer time.

- **1)** As an alternative *Warm Up* activity where you are confident that everyone has had at least one 'date':

- Ask each person to fill in, anonymously, the following questions about their first date:

    a) What was your age at the time?
    b) What was the age of your boy/girlfriend?
    c) Where did you go?
    d) How long did the relationship last?

- Collect in and redistribute the papers and get people to read out the papers they now have. If there is a possibility of people being embarrassed by having their paper recognised, you may wish to read out the papers, or a sample of them, yourself.

- **2)** Display an acetate/poster with two sections headed: JESUS and CHURCH. Discuss ways in which Jesus shows his love for the Church and write these on the acetate/poster. Then think of ways in which the Church shows its submission to Jesus and add these. Now label the same sections at the bottom with: HUSBAND and WIFE and get someone to read **Ephesians 5:21-33**. Point out that this is the kind of relationship within which God wants sex to be expressed. There can hardly be a more positive one!

- **3)** In **1 Corinthians 7:1-9**, Paul recognises the strength of sexual feelings and sees the need to express them within marriage as right and proper. Discuss how the themes of '*love*' and '*submission*' described in **Ephesians 5:21-33** relate to sexual behaviour inside marriage.

GROUP EXTRA

DIRE CONSEQUENCES

Macho Marvin met Flirtatious Freda at An All Night Party when she'd had too much to drink. He said to her: 'How'd you like to come upstairs?' She said to him: 'Now there's an offer I can't refuse.'

The consequence was:
An unwanted pregnancy.

Sleep-around Sid met Virgin Veronica at the school disco when all her mates were sexually experienced. He said to her: 'You don't know what you're missing.' She said to him: 'Perhaps you'd better show me.'

The consequence was:
H.I.V. positive.

Salesman Stan met Bored Bertha at the P.T.A. meeting when her husband was away on business. He said to her: 'What's an attractive lady like you doing on her own?' She said to him: 'Flattery will get you everywhere.'

The consequence was:
Another increase in the divorce statistics.

SESSION 5

Any Dream Won't Do – Other Faiths

Teaching Point

That there is one God and that Jesus Christ is the only way to God.

Group Action

Members to respect other religions while understanding that Jesus Christ is unique and the only way to God.

Getting Ready

This session could become complex and confusing, so make sure you keep it simple enough for your young people to understand. You may like to branch out into a more theological discussion (briefly), to show the depths of Christianity, or take some of your more serious minded young people to one side for more in depth and thought-provoking study. Whatever you do though, don't turn young people off by your love of thorny issues. Tackle it at their level, not yours.

The Key Difference

Salvation is the undeserved gift of God which was obtained for us by the death and resurrection of Jesus Christ. There is no other way to God and it is this which makes the difference between Christianity and other religions.

Biblical references:

Jonah 2:9
   Comes from the Lord

Romans 1:16 and 17
   Is for everyone who believes

Acts 4:12
   Is in Christ alone

Matthew 1:21
   Is saving from sin

John 3:17 and 18
   Is Christ saving not condemning the world

1 Timothy 2:3-5
   God wants for everyone

1 Timothy 1:15
   Is Christ saving sinners

The above references can be used in *Second Half* when small groups should consider the following questions:

> What are we saved from?
> How are we saved?
> Who saves us?

These are just a few passages, but there are plenty of other references you could use – look up 'Saves', 'Salvation', 'Saviour', etc. in the concordance.

Equipment

- ✓ Bibles, notebooks, pens, *Group Extra* sheets
- ✓ OHP/screen or posters/roll of paper
- ✓ OHP pens/acetate or marker pens
- ✓ Material to decorate your meeting room to look like Heaven
- ✓ Cut-out cloud tags with verses written on them
- ✓ Blu-tak

Music

We Believe In God The Father
Meekness And Majesty
You Are The King Of Glory
I Am The Bread Of Life

Team Talk

Leading discussions well is very hard. Consider the group dynamics of a group of 40 compared with those of a group of 5. Keep your eyes open for signs of people wanting to speak but do not have the confidence to break in. Pay very close attention to the questions you ask. Make sure they aren't dead ends, or impossible to answer, or embarrassingly easy, and keep your eyes open for boredom. You may be fascinated by the subject, but are your group? Keep discussions short and stop while they still want more.

First Half looks at this from the 'How do you get to Heaven?' viewpoint.

Second Half looks at it from the 'What is Salvation?' viewpoint. (i.e. to put it negatively, if Salvation is about feeling good and fulfilled, then many religions will give you Salvation and therefore Pluralism is an acceptable way of life).

Particularly when looking at salvation, stress as much as possible that our salvation is *God's* work from beginning to end.

As people arrive, give them a cloud shaped tag with one of the verses from *First Half* written on one side. You will need these tags later on. Then try:

▓ TASTE THE DIFFERENCE

▓ Before the meeting, place cans of drink around your meeting room, with the sides of the can covered in paper to disguise it. Number each can.

▓ Or purchase different brands of cornflakes from local shops, and have bowls of cornflakes around the meeting room. Number the bowls. Give each member a straw or spoon and ask them to identify the cans of drink/cornflakes.

▓ Once they have realised that the drinks/cornflakes all taste similar, explain that pluralism is the belief that all religions are, underneath the packaging the same. Some would say that all religions lead to God and are therefore basically identical. This session sets out to show that Christianity is unique among religions. It is the Shredded Wheat of breakfast cereals and the Irn Bru amongst cans of drink.

▓ NAME THAT TUNE

▓ If you and/or your group are remotely musical, teach them a new song and even try to get them to sing it in parts. Once they have got this and are singing it reasonably well, get one or two other people to sing a completely different song at the same time. Show your group that pluralism believes that all religions sing the same song, whereas evangelical Christians believe that we sing a significantly different song from the other religions.

▓ DEFINITIONS

▓ Ask your group to define Pluralism. Either give them a list of suggestions (silly and serious) to choose from, or ask them to give you two definitions, one silly, one serious on slips of paper. Divide your group into threes, collect and re-distribute the slips, and have them read out. Then the groups of three decide which is the best silly definition and the best serious definition.

You will need to introduce the term 'Pluralism' and define it if you haven't already done this in the *Warm Up*.

▓ The Concise Oxford Dictionary defines Pluralism as "A system that recognises more than one ultimate principle". So religious Pluralism is a system which recognises more than one god, and could be expanded to include a religious system which recognises a variety of ways of reaching this God or gods.

▓ It results in vague and often very general beliefs.

First Half and *Second Half* look at the same material but from different angles. Make sure you do *First Half*. If you have time and want to go into more depth, do *Second Half* too. Don't just do *Second Half*.

▓ *First Half* looks at the question of what Christianity says about how you get to Heaven. *Second Half* looks at the question of what is meant by Salvation.

■ AGREE OR DISAGREE?

■ Label one end of your meeting room 'Agree', and the other end 'Disagree'. Then read out the following statements. Members must decide whether they agree/disagree and then go to the appropriate side of the room:

- ⇨ I like chocolate
- ⇨ Ford Escorts are great cars
- ⇨ Red is a great colour for a sweatshirt
- ⇨ All nice people go to Heaven
- ⇨ There will be no pets in Heaven
- ⇨ Only Christianity can get you to Heaven
- ⇨ It doesn't matter what you believe as long as you are sincere
- ⇨ Only Christianity can tell you the truth about God

■ Add in other statements as you wish. Play this game in a more sedate manner if you wish by writing down the answers. Explain that Pluralism says all religions are equally valid, so you could go to Heaven if you are a Hindu or a Muslim as well as if you are a Christian.

■ Show your group what the Bible and, in particular, what Jesus Christ, say about this matter.

■ Refer to the cloud tags they were given as they came in and ask them to join up with others with the same Bible verse or passage. The cloud tags should have the following verses, 1 per tag:

1 John 5:11-13   John 20:30 and 31   John 11:25 and 26
John 14:1-7   1 Peter 2:4-6   Luke 23:43

■ Ask the group to look up their passage and see what it says about how to get to Heaven and who gets to Heaven. Put up on the overhead projector or a poster 'How do you get to Heaven and who goes there?' and ask them to write in no more than ten words, their answer to this either on a small piece of acetate or on another piece of paper which you can blu-tak to the poster. If using acetate, make sure each piece is small enough to be able to get all contributions on to the screen at the same time.

■ **Summarise the main points.**

- ⇨ **1.** God wants everyone to go to Heaven.
- ⇨ **2.** The Bible is clear that some will not make it.
- ⇨ **3.** Jesus himself is exclusive.
  He said that no-one gets to Heaven apart from Him.

Run a supermarket of different faiths.

HALF TIME

■ Write out briefing cards on the different faiths for each 'shopkeeper' and give them each a small pile of slips with the name of their faith. Allow time for them to assimilate the information you have given them, and then each shopkeeper has to stand on a chair and, as in a street market, they have to advertise their wares.

■ Members circulate and may take up to five slips of paper from each shopkeeper, depending on how well they have sold their faith, and how convincing their argument is.

■ Members may not collect more than a total of five slips of paper. Allow members to circulate and choose and then collect the slips of paper they want.

■ At the end, either see which shopkeeper has most/least slips of paper left and/or see what members have collected.

■ Make the point that if Christianity is true, it is pointless collecting any slips from any of the other faiths.

This approaches the question of Pluralism from a different view point and looks at the question of what Salvation is.

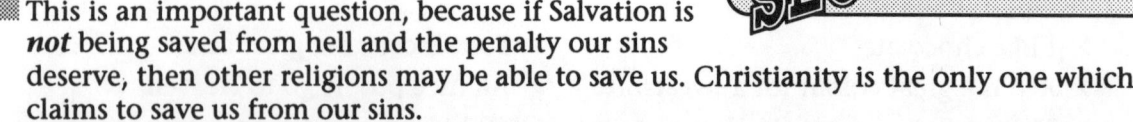

- This is an important question, because if Salvation is *not* being saved from hell and the penalty our sins deserve, then other religions may be able to save us. Christianity is the only one which claims to save us from our sins.

- You could look at this by either giving a straight talk on **Ephesians 2:1-10**, or using the material in 'All Together Forever' published by and available from CPAS or COVENANTERS. Note that **Ephesians 2:1-3** talks about our position before we are saved, and **Ephesians 2:4-10** about our position after we are saved. The emphasis is that it is God who saves us. It is his work, not ours, and only He can do this because Salvation is Salvation from sin and its consequences (**V.1-3**).

- Alternatively you could look at a variety of biblical verses on Salvation by dividing into groups to look up the verses and answer the questions as set out in *Getting Ready*.

- Stress that biblically salvation is from sin and that Jesus Christ is the only one who can do this. Dispel the idea that salvation is anything else such as finding yourself becoming a whole person, being one with God, etc. and show that because salvation is salvation from sin, then there is only one religion, indeed one person, in history who could do this.

Use this last part to help members think about their response, and to think about other religions.

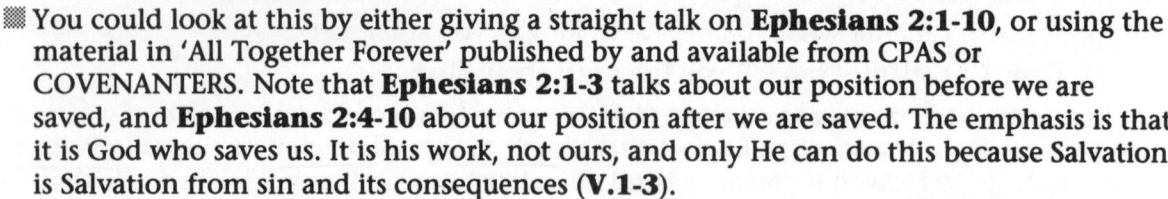

- Explain that the Bible talks about general revelation. Tell your group that God reveals himself to people through creation (see **Romans 1**) and through their conscience. But also say that people will be judged according to how they have responded to the revelation that God has given them. And at the end of the day God is just (see **Genesis 18:25**).

- Either make these points in a short talk or lead a discussion.

- Give the members time to respond personally to God. Pray together, thanking God for his revelation, asking Him to help us think through these things, and praying for those who have never heard of Jesus Christ, God's greatest revelation.

▓ DECORATIONS

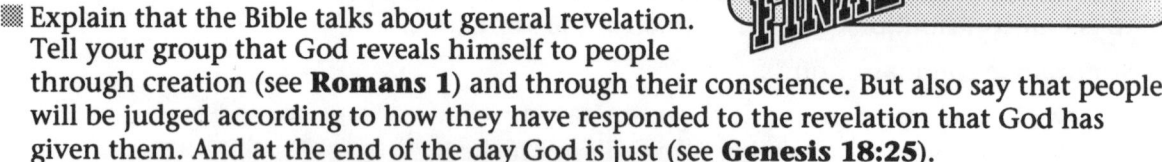

- As this meeting is about who will go to heaven, you could decorate your meeting room to look like Heaven. Have large cut out clouds and angels attached to the ceiling. Use copious amounts of cotton wool and bubble blowing, even a smoke machine. Have one leader play Peter and welcome the members at the pearly door as they arrive.

▓ WHO?

- As the *Warm Up*, or in the *First Half*, ask 'Who?'. Take copies of the chart headed 'Heaven Bound' from *Group Extra*. Ask members to rate each grouping from 1-7 for goodness (above the line), and from 1-7 for their chance of going to Heaven (below the line). Lead into a discussion on this subject.

GROUP EXTRA

GROUPINGS	HEAVEN BOUND
ENGLISH	1 |—————————————————| 7
JEW	1 |—————————————————| 7
FOOTBALL SUPPORTER	1 |—————————————————| 7
MUSLIM	1 |—————————————————| 7
CARPENTER	1 |—————————————————| 7
CHRISTIAN	1 |—————————————————| 7
SIKH	1 |—————————————————| 7
CAR MECHANIC	1 |—————————————————| 7
HINDU	1 |—————————————————| 7

SESSION 6

Colour Blind – Racism

Teaching Point

To understand why racism is wrong.

Group Action

Aim that members will change their thinking about racial minorities, and begin to act more positively towards them.

Getting Ready

1) There could be a reasonable amount of up-front monologue in this session. That is fine, but do make sure it is well illustrated, both verbally and physically.

2) Make sure your members can trust you. If the Private Diaries idea is going to work well, they must be private, and it is your responsibility to make sure that they are. Don't embarrass people and betray their trust by a public exposure of something they thought was for their consumption only.

3) God needs to speak to us before we can be really effective at communicating his truth to others. It will be a powerful example if you can point to something in your life that has changed as a result of preparing for this session.

Philippians 2: 1-4

- The reason for Christian behaviour is that we are united with Christ (**v 1**).

- Because we have the Spirit, we are called to have the same love as Christ (**v 2**) and to behave as he did (**v 1**).

- Specifically, we should :

    1) Consider others better than ourselves (**v 3**).

    2) Look to the interests of others (**v 4**).

    V 3 and **v 4** are very important. Why not learn these as a group, or even make bookmarks or posters with these verses at the top? This could be done as part of this session.

Ask your group what these verses mean when applied to people of other races.

James 2:1-13

Racists show favouritism to their own race. Favouritism is out for the Christian, and this passage tells us why:

1) Favouritism is out because of the nature of God (**vv 1-7**). He is the Lord of Glory (**v 1**), and he has a place for the poor (**vv 5-7**).

2) Favouritism is out because of the law of God (**vv 8-11**).

3) Favouritism is out because of the judgement of God (**vv 12,13**).

Equipment

- ✓ Bibles, notebooks, pens, *Group Extra* sheets
- ✓ OHP/sheet of card and pens
- ✓ Magazines/Newspapers/Glue/Scissors
- ✓ Material to make bookmarks/posters
- ✓ Record Cards
- ✓ Paper for private diaries

Music

Let There Be Love Shared Among Us

Bind Us Together Lord

For I'm Building A People Of Power

A New Commandment

Jesus Put This Song Into Our Hearts

Team Talk

This teaching session aims to show group members why racism is wrong for the Christian.

First Half concentrates on some of the reasons why we should treat other human beings well.

Second Half looks more deeply at the Church, seeking to understand what God has done for us in Jesus Christ, breaking down the dividing wall of hostility which separates people one from another.

Young people may instinctively feel that racism is wrong. Use this session to help them think this through more and to understand why it is wrong.

Select one of the following:

■ 1. DEFINITIONS

■ Ask your group to define racism. Use one of a variety of ways, depending on their 'intellectualism':

    a) Simply ask them to write a definition, and then discuss it.

    b) Ask them to write down a definition, collect them in a hat, then read them out (anonymously), and decide on marks out of 25 for each one.

    c) Give your group a variety of possible definitions, and ask them to choose the best.

■ The Concise Oxford Dictionary defines racism as "The tendency to racial feeling, antagonism between different races of men."

■ Racial discrimination has been defined as "Legal or social disadvantages imposed by men of one race on those of another", and racism as "The belief that one race is superior to another".

■ 2. WORD ASSOCIATION

■ Try a word association with words such as these for prompts:

■ West Indian, French, black, curry, Italian, Pakistani, pasta, Chinese, Xavier, Antonio, Asif, Ugandan, etc.

■ Intersperse these words with more passive words. Either ask people to shout out the first word that comes into their head, or to write it down. The important thing is that people's responses are instant and spontaneous, and that they don't have time to think about them.

■ 3. SPOILED FOR CHOICE

■ Divide into groups of 3-4, and give each group a selection of magazines and newspapers. Ask them to search through and cut out references to, or pictures of, people in racial minorities, and to construct a visual display. Comment on the variety in our world, and see how many of the references are about racial abuse and discrimination.

By reinforcing what has been covered in the *Warm Up*, and by explaining what racism is, and that in this session, we will be seeing why it is out for the Christian.

In *First Half*, look at some of the rules for Christian living, which are particularly relevant for how we treat people of other races.

    ■ **a)** Using the outline on **Philippians 2:1-4** from *Getting Ready*, either give a straight talk, or draw out the main points by asking questions.

■ b) PRIVATE DIARIES (1)

■ Ask group members to keep a private diary of this evening. Give them a record card at this point and ask them to note down confidentially what they think about what they have just read from the Bible. This could be given out at the start of the session, for them to confidentially write down what they feel about other races, and then to see how this changes through the evening. Ask them to add to their private diary later on in the session (in *Second Half* and *Final Whistle*).

▪ **c)** Depending on time, you may like to look at **James 2:1-13** which focusses on favouritism.

▪ Give this as a straight input, using the details from *Getting Ready*, or simply introduce a Bible discussion by asking "What does this teach about racism and the Christian?"

Play:

▪ YES/NO/DON'T KNOW

HALF TIME

▪ Cut up the series of statements under this heading from *Group Extra*. On one side of your meeting room attach 3 pieces of paper, 'Yes', 'No', and 'Don't Know', which form headings for three columns.

▪ Give group members in turn one of the statements and a piece of Blu-tak, and they take it in turns to go up to the wall and attach their statements in the appropriate column. With a larger group, split into 2 or more teams and make this a race.

▪ Discuss the results with your group.

▪ FAMILY TREES

▪ If you suspect that it may produce good results, (i.e. reveal peoples multi-racial backgrounds), then ask members to draw their family trees as far back as they can, and see what countries are represented.

▪ You could ask them to do this the week before, enlisting some family help, and bring the results with them to the meeting.

▪ See who in your group is for example, ½ Irish, ⅛ Scottish, ¹⁄₁₆ French, ¼ West Indian, etc. Ask your group if this knowledge about certain members alters their opinions of their friends.

This looks at **Ephesians 2:14-22**, and shows how God has broken down, by the cross, barriers between us and others, and between us and God. This shows how, in the Church, there is one new society, and therefore no room for racism of any sort.

SECOND HALF

▪ Divide your group into pairs, and ask each pair to look at these questions about the passage:

   1) How has Jesus' death broken down the dividing wall of hostility between people?

   2) What are the positive results of Jesus' death?

   3) What difference should this make to the way we live with others in the church?

▪ To illustrate this passage, you could use an OHP with permanent and water-soluble pens. Ask your group to brainstorm the different pairs of racial groups where there is a traditional barrier, and write these on the OHP in permanent ink. Then with a broad water-soluble pen, draw in the dividing walls between people, and refer to **V 14**. Through the cross though, these walls have been broken down. Wipe your acetate with a damp cloth to remove the walls, and draw another one around the outside if you wish. Refer to **V 14** again to show what Jesus has done.

■ PRIVATE DIARIES (2)

■ If you are doing this, remember to ask members to put their thoughts from *Second Half* down in their private diaries now.

Ask your members to write down the names of some of the people they know who come from racial minorities.

FINAL WHISTLE

■ Then, confidentially, ask them to note down one or two things that they should change in the way they think about those people, and one or two things they could do to improve their actions towards those people. Challenge them at least to begin to do something about their actions in the next 36 hours. And then pray together about what has been written down.

■ PRIVATE DIARIES (3)

■ If you are doing this, remember to ask members to put in their final entry for this evening, asking them to write down what they intend to think and do as a result.

■ 1) INTERVIEW

■ If you know a black Christian, ask them along to this meeting, and interview them about what it's like being black in a predominantly white country, and how they, as a Christian, cope with it.

EXTRA TIME

■ 2) TENSION GETTER

■ Try this, to reveal people's attitudes on race:

> "You like curry, and you like Indians. But 9 Indians have just moved in next door. They speak a language you don't understand, keep themselves to themselves, and cook a lot of curry. Somehow, other people's currys don't smell very nice, and in the summer the smell fills your small garden, and if you leave the doors or windows open, it fills your house as well. The women next door don't come to the door, and the men work all hours at the local corner shop, so it's hard to talk to them about the problem. Your father hates them, and your mother isn't much better. Now your older brother, who comes to the church youth group with you and makes the right Christian noises, joins in the abuse of the 'Curry Kitchen'. What should you say to him?"

GROUP EXTRA

YES / NO / DON'T KNOW

STATEMENT	YES	NO	?
* West Indians commit more crime per head than English people?			
* Black people just want to live off the state?			
* All Italians are noisy and lazy?			
* Black people can't speak English?			
* Racism is not a problem here?			
* Indians are more intelligent than Europeans?			
* French people have no manners?			
* Brixton just isn't like England at all?			
* Pakistani's keep themselves to themselves, so we shouldn't interfere?			
* Coloured people can't be English?			
* People who come to live here should adopt our culture?			

SESSION 7

I Was Hungry And You Held A Concert – Famine

Teaching Point

That famine is ultimately attributable to sin. As Christians we should be striving to demonstrate God's redeeming work by alleviating the effects and removing the causes of famine.

Group Action

To express our concern about the causes and effects of famine in practical ways.

PRE-MATCH

Getting Ready

Famine has become too familiar to us all in recent years. As a result, there is the danger of us and our young people being affected by 'compassion fatigue' – we can't cope emotionally with any more appeals for aid, so we eventually give up responding.

Added to this, there is the growing frustration that, for all the efforts of Band Aid and its sequels, for all the millions of pounds raised, and for all the media coverage, nothing seems to have changed significantly – famine still happens and, if anything, appears to be spreading in Africa.

This leads on to a feeling of helplessness when faced with the enormity of the problem. The whole thing is far too big for my tiny efforts to make any difference whatsoever, so why bother any more?

The problem of famine is not a new one. The Bible has plenty to say on the subject. The word 'famine' itself appears almost one hundred times and there are nine separate occasions, referred to in the Old Testament, when famine occurred. Some of these will be well known, like the seven year famine at the time of Joseph (**Genesis 41-47**) and the three years of drought and famine prophesied by Elijah during the reign of Ahab (**1 Kings 17-18**).

Whatever we might feel about the 'burden' of famine, it pales into insignificance when set alongside the feelings of those going through it.

Equipment

- ✓ Bibles, notebooks, pens, *Group Extra* sheets
- ✓ OHP/screen or posters/roll of paper
- ✓ OHP pens/acetate or marker pens
- ✓ Paper pens/pencils
- ✓ Group Bible study passages and questions
- ✓ Cartoon by Taffy photocopied or on acetate
- ✓ Information on proposed practical project

Music

He Has Showed You, O Man
Soften My Heart
Who Can Sound The Depths Of Sorrow

Team Talk

Much of the attention normally given to this subject tends to focus on the specific problems of the areas currently affected, the immediate response needed to deal with it, and maybe some longer-term measures aimed at prevention. Not much thought is given to a Biblical perspective on the issue, partly because it is not an easy one to tackle.

Our aim is to do that, which may raise some uncomfortable questions.

First Half looks at what the Bible has to say on the subject.

Second Half looks at what our response should be.

WARM UP

Hand out copies of 'I Have No Food', ask the group to look at each of the reasons and decide whether they are: G – God's responsibility; P – people's responsibility; or C – a combination of the two. This can be done either individually, followed by a report back, or as a group. Watch out for non-readers.

KICK OFF

Reproduce and discuss the cartoon by Taffy on page 44. (Reproduced with permission from Tear Fund). List the group members' comments on a poster/acetate.

FIRST HALF

Famine is often seen as a 'natural disaster', caused by drought, floods, or pests, such as locusts, but the list of reasons the group has just read show that many of the worst effects are people's responsibility. What does the Bible have to say on the subject?

- Either work through each of these passages briefly together or divide into smaller teams and give each one a passage to read and investigate. (Put the questions on the OHP/roll of paper or give handouts to the groups).

- **Genesis 3:17-19** What happened to the earth? Why? What effect would this have?

- The passage shows that the very ground itself is cursed because of sin. Instead of the abundant provision in Eden, growing crops for food would now be people's future means of survival, but it would be a problematic one.

- **Genesis 4:10-12** Ask the same questions as above.

- These verses tell how the ground would fail to produce crops for Cain as a consequence of his murdering his brother, Able. Even 'natural disasters' are linked to sin and, therefore, people's responsibility. This thought is further developed by the prophets who attribute famine to God's judgement on sin.

- **2 Samuel 21:1** What problem did David experience? Where did he look for an answer? What was the cause of the problem? In this instance, famine was the result of sin previously committed by Saul against the Gibeonites.

- **Jeremiah 15:1-4 V.2** speaks of God's judgement in four ways, what are they? According to **V 4**, whose fault was this? Now look at **2 Kings 21:1-16** to find out what he had done.

- Summarise the findings of the group on a sheet of paper or O.H.P. acetate, bringing out the following points:

    1) All problems of nature are ultimately caused by sin.

    2) Sometimes specific problems can be linked directly to the sin of individuals or groups of people.

    3) These problems can be evidence of God's judgement against sin.

    4) It is not always just those who sinned who suffer the effects.

- Finally, point out that the linking of famine with judgement on sin is not made in every case. Where the link is made, it comes as a warning of coming judgement in order to turn people from sin. It is never presented as an explanation for famine after the event.

HALF TIME

Look again at the *Group Extra* sheet. Get the group to look at the reasons for famine which they had identified as people's responsibility. In each case, try to name the specific cause which lies behind the reason given, e.g. greed, selfishness, corruption, war, ignorance, pride, etc.

▩ Ask these questions:

1) Are people starving because they are lazy?
2) Do rich countries like the U.K. help, or do they make matters worse?

SECOND HALF

What should our response to famine be? In *Second Half* there are a number of passages which can be looked at all together or in smaller groups.

▩ Alongside the theme of judgement, we also find references to God's protection during times of famine. Despite years of personal suffering, Joseph's testimony to his brothers was, "God sent me ahead of you to preserve for you a remnant on earth and to save your lives by a great deliverance." (**Genesis 45:7**)

▩ **Psalm 33:18-19**

On whose behalf does God act in famine?

▩ **Psalm 37:18-19**

▩ **1 Kings 17:7-16**

How did God provide for Elijah during the famine? How did the people concerned benefit?

▩ **Romans 8:35**

What can famine not do?

▩ Several passages deal with responses to hunger and famine. We have the action of Jesus himself, borne out of compassion, in feeding the crowds (**Matthew 14:13-21**) and we have the illustration of the 'sheep' and 'goats' as a picture of God's judgement on those who fail to act compassionately to those in physical need.
Then there is the description in **Acts 11:27-30** of how a prophetic message of coming famine in Judah moved the church at Antioch to send aid to their fellow believers.

▩ **Matthew 14:13-21**

How did Jesus feel towards the crowds? How did he respond? Jesus was moved by compassion, which led him to take action to feed the crowd.

▩ **Matthew 25:31-46**

What was the difference between those who received God's blessing and those who were condemned? God's blessing or judgement are here seen as dependant on our acting on behalf of the needy or failing to do so.

▩ **Acts 11:27-30**

How did the Christians at Antioch know about the coming famine?
How did they respond?
What determined how much help they gave?
Their awareness of the coming famine came through a prophetic message, i.e. God warned them in advance. In response, the Christians at Antioch took action to meet the need of their fellow believers in Judea, each according to his ability.

Summarise, once again, the points discovered, emphasising in particular that God *cares* about the victims of famine, He *loves* even in the midst of famine, He *provides* for His people, but He uses other people to do so.

FINAL WHISTLE

- Perhaps give your group members the three key words, in bold above, and get them to say why they think they are so important in summarizing the passages.

- Encourage your group to memorise **James 2:15-17**.

- Discuss practical projects which your church may already be supporting and encourage the group to get involved, OR set up your own group initiative to support a project through TEAR Fund, Oasis or similar organisations. Addresses are given on page 64.

Try these:

EXTRA TIME

- **1)** Design a series of 'road signs' warning of the various events preceding Christ's coming, as listed in **Matthew 24:4-14**. Discuss the Christian's responsibility in **Matthew 24:36-51**. The warning here is for Christians to be ready for His return by being alert and active in His service, part of which must undoubtedly be our response to the victims of famine.

- **2)** Promote an awareness campaign on issues concerning trade, aid, debt, etc. affecting developing countries.

- **3)** Suggest ways of influencing government policy by letter writing to: local M.P.'s, Minister for Overseas Development, Prime Minister, etc.

Reproduced with kind permission from Tear Fund

GROUP EXTRA

Group:	I have no food!
Leader:	Why can't you grow some?
1st Reason:	There hasn't been any rain to make the crops grow.
2nd Reason:	I haven't got any land - it's all owned by the rich men.
3rd Reason:	My land is flooded.
4th Reason:	My good soil has been washed away because too many trees were cut down.
5th Reason:	I have no seed - we were forced to eat it last year when we had no food.
6th Reason:	I did grow enough but locusts came and ate it all.
7th Reason:	My country is at war and I had to flee from my home and leave my crops.
8th Reason:	I have had no food for a long time. Now I am too weak to do farming.
9th Reason:	My government says I have to grow coffee to sell to Europe instead of corn to feed my family.
Leader:	Why can't you buy some?
1st Reason:	There wasn't much rain, so the crops were poor. The price went up, so I can't afford it.
2nd Reason:	I can only get work for 4 months a year. I just don't have enough money to last me.
3rd Reason:	Government policies have led to high inflation, so the shops keep putting up prices and I am left behind.
4th Reason:	My child was ill and I spent all my money on medicines that the adverts said were good. He died anyway.
5th Reason:	All the grain produced around here is being bought up to feed cattle in America. There's none left for me to buy.
6th Reason:	There is no unemployment or supplementary benefit here.
Leader:	Won't someone give you some?
1st Reason:	No one knows we need it - we haven't been on the Nine O'Clock News!
2nd Reason:	Our government won't admit there is a problem - it would make them look foolish.
3rd Reason:	There is a war on and the armies won't let the food through to us.
4th Reason:	Corrupt officials are stealing the food before it reaches us.
5th Reason:	Our government can't afford to help - they are repaying their debts to Western banks and governments.
6th Reason:	Foreign governments won't send any because they don't like our government.
Leader:	Famine needn't happen! There is enough food to feed all the people in the world. But it's not shared out fairly. And some people just can't get any.
Group:	I have no food!

SESSION 8

Watch It With Your Eyes Open – The Media

Teaching Point

The Media exerts a large, and possibly negative, influence on a Christian.

Group Action

Aim that the group should begin to develop the ability to critically assess the media they 'consume' and adjust their consumption of it accordingly.

PRE-MATCH

Getting Ready

What should the Biblical response to the Media be? Try the following outline for a brief talk:

(a) Be Aware

Don't assume all the media is 'fit for Christian consumption'. Make sure your group keep their eyes open and think about it. It may be anti-Christian material which they are consuming. It can spread stereotypes which are unhelpful to Christians, and the subtle un-Christian or anti-Christian messages can be very persuasive.

(b) Be Biblical

Focus on **Philippians 4**, and first look at **vs11,12 & 19**. From these, teach about Paul's learning to be content. Advertising agencies would never have this as their motto....

Second, look at **v8**, and teach the importance of fixing your minds on the good things, rather than on the dubious. What Christians think about is very important, and the media influences our thinking a good deal. What goes into our minds controls our thinking, so be positive too, and teach the importance of Christian input to our minds. Use **Romans 12:1,2** to teach the importance of renewing our minds.

Third, the media throws into question where our treasure should be stored up. The media pampers to human greed, so a careful study of **Matthew 6:20,21** would be valuable, focussing on the impermanence and frailty of earthly goods compared with heavenly goods, and the dangerous effect which earthly goods have on our hearts.

Fourth, careful study of **Colossians 3:1-11** will be valuable. You may choose to establish first some principles of Christian living: that it starts with the fact of what Christ has achieved for us (**vs 3**), so we have our hearts and minds set in the right place (**vv1,2**); and all the Christian life is lived in the shadow of the future coming of Christ (**vs 4**).

With this in mind, then, we can begin to be practical, putting to death and ridding ourselves of all that belongs to our sinful nature (**vv 5 ff**). Then ask your group (perhaps in three's?) to consider what this has to say about our media consumption, and ask them to be as specific and detailed as possible: no vague generalities allowed ...

(c) Be Cautious

Point out that the media consumes a great deal of precious time. Ask how it could be used more productively for God. Ask what Christians' priorities should be in their use of time. Note too that the influence of the media can be slow, subtle and invidious, changing Christian minds so that they think the same way the world does. Get your group thinking: 'What is the media doing to me?' Stress now that we need to 'watch the media with our eyes open'.

Equipment

✓ *Group Extra* sheets
✓ OHP/sheet of card and pens
✓ Copies of a variety of newspaper reports of the same incident
✓ Video snippets of adverts
✓ Video snippets of soap opera introductions
✓ Magazine adverts
✓ TV/videos (if using it)

Music

Take My Life & Let It Be
I Want To Worship The Lord With All Of My Heart
The Greatest Thing In All My Life....

Team Talk

Young people can get a lot of negative input from Christians about the media. In this session try and be positive as well as negative. Media influence on us is not all bad, there are good elements too, although we do need to keep our eyes open to the unhelpful and negative influences.

It's also very easy to look at the media but not look at it Christianly. So as you select and adapt from this material, make sure all the Bible material is included, and throughout this session, clearly focus the need to view the media from a Christian perspective. Try not to be trapped into purely informing about the media, but instead help our young people to think and act in a Christian manner where the media is concerned.

WARM UP

Ask your group to think up some obscure fact about themselves which no-one else in the group knows, and then turn this into a newspaper headline: perhaps a tabloid headline.

▨ Ask them to write this down on a slip of paper and then get one of the leaders to write the headlines onto the OHP/large sheet of card. Ask the rest of the group to decide which headline refers to which person within the group.

KICK OFF

By outlining what the media is, and which aspects you will be focussing on in this week's session.

▨ This material looks at the influence of TV/radio, newspapers, magazines and adverts in general. You may want to draw examples from just one of these, or take material from other areas such as films, books, etc.

FIRST HALF

Emphasise that the media is a very strong influence on us, and that this influence can be negative and unhelpful for the Christian, but needn't necessarily be so.

▨ (A) THE INFLUENCE OF THE MEDIA

▨ Stress that the media is a very strong influence on most of us because of the amount we consume, and the power of it. Ask your group individually to fill in a copy of the media consumption chart (see *Group Extra*). Then compare notes and prepare to be amazed at the amount that we consume. Compare your group's results with the average U.K. weekly media consumption of 75 hours per person. Other statistics include the fact that 5-14 year olds spend an average of 23 hours per week watching the television, so that by their late teens they have witnessed 16,000 violent deaths on the screen.

▨ The proliferation of satellite dishes and cable TV means a far wider choice of viewing, and the increasing number of televisions and videos means that programmes can be recorded and watched several times at the viewer's convenience. You may like to ask how many of your group have one, two or three televisions in their house, and one, two or three VCRs. And make it clear before you ask that multiple ownership isn't necessarily something to be proud of.

▨ Second, stress the power of the media, and especially that the media is not only part of our society, but it actually changes society. The media affects what we buy, how we spend our time, what is important to us, what we eat and drink, etc. Newspapers not only reflect public opinion, they shape it.

▨ There are plenty of examples to draw from our own experience here. One particularly good one is the way that the Smirnoff Vodka advertising campaign, targeted at making Vodka an acceptable drink for younger people, has actually changed people's drinking habits so much that vodka is now a common drink for many in their 20's and 30's.

▨ The media also becomes part of our everyday language. Show your group this by giving them the following advertising slogans verbally, or on a hand-out, or visually on a card/OHP. Then ask them to match the company or product with the slogan. They'll probably find it very easy.

1. "Vorsprung durch tecnik."
2. "Once driven, forever smitten."
3. "The world's favourite airline."
4. "Reaches the parts ..."
5. "We're getting there."
6. "We are. Are you?"
7. "Let your fingers do the walking."
8. "The mild cigar, from..."
9. "It's you we answer to."
10. "I know a man who can."

▓ Some of these may now be out of date, so replace them with more contemporary ones.

(B) THE NEGATIVE INFLUENCE THE MEDIA CAN HAVE

▓ Show your group some adverts. Cut them out of magazines or newspapers, or if you can, video a selection from the television.

Ask your group:

⇨ What kind of message do they portray? (An ideal world? Greed? Materialism? I'll be O.K. if I have this product? I'll be accepted if I have this product?)

⇨ Give examples of how sex is used in advertising? (Many adverts use sex to sell their products. That's not what God intended sex to be for!)

⇨ What unspoken communication is going on? (The media says much more than is spoken, and much of this is very powerful.)

⇨ How realistic a view do these give of what the world is really like? (Many adverts give a distorted and idealised view of the world, and so distort people's perception of reality.)

▓ This distortion of reality is common to all the media. It is partly due to the fact that unbiased reporting is impossible. The reporter/advert maker/programme maker is bound to influence us by their own thoughts and ideas, their choice of words, by the camera angle, etc. But some distortion is intended. To show this, buy several different, contrasting newspapers, and cut out their reports of the same event. Pin these reports together, and give each collection of reports to your group to see how differently newspapers treat an article. Ask your group why this is the case, and then discuss the power which the media can have on us, and whether these reports are actually truthful.

HALF TIME

Give your group a selection of magazine adverts, watch some pre-recorded television, or listen to the radio, again pre-recorded, and using the chart below, ask your group which of the following values were mentioned in the excerpts.

▓ (Tick each one as many times as it is mentioned).

Values mentioned/referred to	No. of times	Values mentioned/referred to	No. of times
1. Wealth, luxury, greed		8. Responsibility	
2. Security		9. Ego/pride	
3. Sex or physical attractiveness		10. Escapism	
4. Intelligence		11. Ease, comfort	
5. Conformity		12. Freedom from responsibility	
6. Justice		13. Status	
7. Power, strength		14. Other	

▓ Discuss the results as a group, and try to draw conclusions about what the media says to us, and whether it's values and influence are helpful or unhelpful for the Christian.

SECOND HALF

Begin the second half by asking your group to fill in chart 2 - 'How you see it' from *Group Extra*. They may need some guidance from you on the 'How the Bible sees it' section. Discuss this together, and remind your group that the media can be a bad influence.

- Ask your group to suggest ways in which the media can be a good influence. The following are some examples:
  - ⇨ The media can highlight wrongs in society and help us remove them. (e.g. child abuse, third world starvation)
  - ⇨ The media can be good entertainment, and there's nothing wrong with that.
  - ⇨ The media helps us use leisure time wisely by relaxing.
  - ⇨ If done well (i.e. well written, well acted), the media can be uplifting.
- Give a talk, using the outline given in *Getting Ready*, about how a Christian should respond to the media.

FINAL WHISTLE

Ask your group to consider how their attitude to the media should change.

- Make practical suggestions such as cutting down on the amount of TV, and using the time more usefully, or suggest a campaign of letter writing to the local or national papers or TV/radio if an issue has arisen in a meeting. Media chiefs do apparently take complaints seriously.
- You may like to instigate a media review in your youth group every so often, where you look at the values and impact of addictive programmes, and assess them from a Christian perspective.
- Ask your group members to make a private written note of one thing which this evening's session will change, and one area where their eyes have been opened and which they will view differently from now on.

EXTRA TIME

- **1.** Election time. Draw up a list of 5 or 6 nominations for each of the following categories:

T.V. Programmes	Videos	Magazines
Newspapers	Films	
Radio D.J.'s	Adverts	

- Ask members to vote for their top three in each category by giving them six votes to be placed, three for the top, two for the second, and one for the third. Use the election to draw up a list of group favourites.
- **2.** In *First Half*, instead of using the advertising slogans, ask a group member to record advertising jingles on TV adverts, but to leave out the product, and ask your group to guess the products. They will probably find it very easy.
- **3.** In *First Half* again, while looking at the negative power of the media, you may want to use a VCR to record the opening moments of several soap operas (starting with the signature tune, but stopping just before the first words are spoken). Ask your group what these excerpts have said so far by the images they have portrayed.

GROUP EXTRA

MY MEDIA CONSUMPTION

TYPE OF MEDIA	HOURS P/W AVERAGE
Television	
Radio	
Newspapers	
Magazines	
Adverts (eg. trains, billboards, etc.)	
Films	
Books	
Other (specify) –	

HOW YOU SEE IT

TOPIC	HOW THE MEDIA SEES IT	HOW THE BIBLE SEES IT
Sex		
The Family		
Success		
Relationships		
Marriage		
God		
Christianity		

SESSION 9

A Twentieth Century God – Materialism

Teaching Point

God gives us things to use for His benefit, not just for ours.

Group Action

Aim that the group will develop a godly attitude towards possessions and begin to use them for God, and especially for the Gospel.

PRE-MATCH

Getting Ready

The temptation with this session is to teach purely about money and how a Christian uses it. This is, however, only an element of the whole area of materialism and so will only be mentioned rather than studied in depth. The aim of this session is to be more general in looking at the issues raised by materialism in the 20th Century.

Materialism consists of the storing up and using of things purely for our own enjoyment and benefit. This is actually idolatry and never satisfies. It is the opposite of what God teaches, in His word, about how we use possessions. Biblically, all we have should be used for God and none of it should be seen as 'mine'. This is covered more fully in *Second Half*.

Luke 16:1-15

V 5-7 – Don't be sidetracked by the dishonesty of the way the shrewd manager deals with his master's debtors.

V 9 – This covers the main point of the parable.

- God wants us to use all our possessions for His purposes.(It isn't 10% for God, 90% for us, but 100% God's).
- God gives us worldly wealth to use to bring others to know Him, and help them to grow in their faith.

Both of these will help to extend the Kingdom of God.

V 11 –

- Trustworthy handling of worldly wealth means to use it for God's glory.
- True riches are the riches of heaven.

This is not an easy passage to grasp, but this understanding of it makes sense of **V 13-15**. There is no change of subject from **V 12** to **13**.

V 13 – This continues the point that we are to use what we have for God, whether it's given away, or spent on possessions which are then used to bring others to God.

V 14 – Here we see that the money-loving Pharisees clearly understood Jesus' meaning, and sneer at him.

V 15 – Finally the end of verse 15 talks of when money and what it can buy is highly valued by men, it is detestable in God's sight.

Use one of these four suggestions for the Bible work in *First Half*:

1) Using a straight talk, ask people to read out the verses at the appropriate time. Focus in on one or two of the passages in **Matthew 6:31-33** and then **1 Timothy 6:6-16**.

2) Divide your group into teams of 4, and give each person in the team a copy of the passages and questions and the task of looking at one of the passages each. Then ask them to report back to the team, having answered the questions on the particular passage chosen.

3) Divide into 4 groups, each group looking at one of the passages and then reporting back to the whole group. At this point, people can make notes of what the others said.

4) Place sheets of paper (A3 or A4) around your meeting room with one of the following headings on each:

'Priorities for the Christian'
'Mistakes we make'
'What is life about?'
'Attitudes to wealth and possessions'
'What eternity has to teach us about our possessions'

Divide your group as outlined in **2)** or **3)** to see what the four passages have to say about these subjects. Then ask group members to write their findings on the relevant sheet.

Equipment

✓ Copies of the *Group Extra* Sheets.
✓ Pen and paper.
✓ Envelopes for time-tokens.
✓ Cut-up time-tokens.
✓ Felt tip pens.
✓ OHP/screen or large sheet of paper and pens.

Music

Seek Ye First The Kingdom Of God
I Want To Serve The Purpose Of God
Take My Life And Let It Be

Team Talk

The *First Half* of the teaching will cover what the Bible has to say negatively about the dangers of materialism and the priorities a Christian should have in the use of their possessions.

The *Second Half* will look more positively at how Christians should view their possessions, including their money.

It is well worth not only thinking through an activity carefully before you do it, but actually trying it out yourself. The time-tokens game, for example, can work very well, but has lots of little pitfalls if it's not carefully thought through and set up well.

WARM UP

Try this as an initial mixer:

- Give someone in your group an amount of money (perhaps a 1 coin, or 5 note), but tell them to keep quiet about this. Then ask group members to circulate, saying hello to each other, and asking for some piece of information, such as their total weekly income, what they spent most on last year, or something less threatening (and less relevant) such as what they had for breakfast. Tell the group that the person with the money will pass it on to the tenth person that they meet, and that person to the tenth person they meet, etc. If you have a small group, you may need to suggest a number of pieces of information to ask of people, to allow several meetings with the same person.

- When you shout stop, find out who has the money, and let them keep it. But ask them to use it to buy biscuits for next week, or some other suitable expenditure.

- If you have more time, try a scavenger hunt. You could let this happen in the hall you meet in, in your home (if you are very brave), or if you have got 30-40 minutes and want a bit more fun, in your local area. The usual scavenger hunts consist in finding a selection of objects, a list of which you can make up from your knowledge of your hall/home/area (one idea would be to collect one item for each letter of the alphabet). This is best done as a competitive team event, even if the teams are only pairs, or there are only two teams.

- If you are really adventurous, and your group would do it, try a scavenger hunt with people as the items to be collected. Give your group points for physically bringing people like the Minister/Elder, a nun, a parent, a policeman, a member of the congregation, a younger brother, an American, etc. to your meeting. Give them 30 minutes. When they come with their friends, welcome the people and invite them to stay for the meeting. Then carry on as normal!

- If your scavenger hunt is for things, it makes a more natural introduction to the meeting, because a scavenger hunt for things is what most people are involved in most of the time, and an obsession with this is called materialism.

KICK OFF

- Begin by defining materialism (see *Getting Ready*), outlining its dangers, and saying how you will be handling this session.

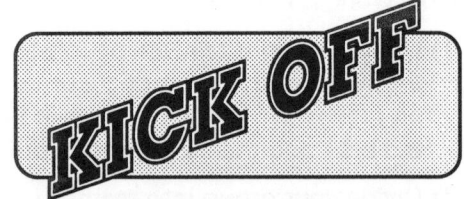

- Make it clear right at the start that in the Bible there are both rich and poor Christians, and that there is nothing wrong with being rich, but it does bring extra responsibilities. The Bible gives warnings to Christians who strive to become rich, but accepts that some will become rich without trying.

FIRST HALF

In this part, there are four Bible passages to use, as you will see below. Before you start, stress to your group that the Bible has many more references to possessions than these, but these are selected references which summarise much of what the Bible is saying.

- You will of course need to have done your homework here, and be prepared to summarise the main points and give guidance where necessary. The **I Timothy 6** passage may be more difficult than the others, so do give it to the older members if you can.

■ THINGS..... AND THE CHRISTIAN

■ Luke 12:13-21
What mistakes did the rich farmer make?
What is his basic problem (see **verse 15**)?
What did the farmer think life was about?
What is life about (**verse 15,21**)?

■ Matthew 6:31-33
What sort of things shouldn't a Christian worry about? (**verse 31**)
What encouragements and promises are here for a Christian?
What are a Christians priorities?
What should a Christian worry about (**verse 33**)?

■ Ecclesiastes 5:10 & 19
What can possessions do?
What can possessions never do?
What should our attitude to them be?
What shouldn't our attitude to them be?

■ I Timothy 6;6-16
What dangers does the love of money lead us into?
What should a Christian's aim in life be?
Why do eternal things encourage us not to love money? (**verses 7,12,13,14**)

■ You could cover these passages in one of the four ways given in *Getting Ready*.

Play 'The Expenditure Game'.

■ From *Group Extra*, photocopy enough sheets for each person in your group. Cut out the money tokens and put one sheet's worth in an envelope and seal it. Do this for each member. Give them the envelopes. Before the meeting, put the following labels around the room:

'Clothes'	'Sweets and food'	'Books'
'Holidays'	'Records'	'Hobbies'
'Alcohol/Cigarettes'	'Transport'	'Give away'
'Entertainment'		

■ By each label put a different coloured felt tip pen. Tell your group members they have £10 to spend (although the tokens in the envelopes add up to more than this to give more flexibility). Ask them to think how they spend their money in an average week, and then to 'spend' their £10 in the same proportion. They spend it by placing it by the appropriate notice, and then shading in the circle on their *Group Extra* sheet appropriately. At the end of the exercise they should have a pie chart of how they spent their money, coloured in with different colours to represent how their money was spent.

■ When all have spent their £10, ask reliable members to add up the total expenditure for each grouping, display this on an OHP or card, and ask members to compare theirs with the overall group result.

■ Discuss the findings, and ask if there are things Christians should or shouldn't do with their money.

SECOND HALF

Focus here on Luke 16:1-15 (see *Getting Ready*). This looks at the positive side of the Christian use of possessions. Ask someone to read this out.

- As this is not an easy passage, a straight talk from one leader may be advisable. If your group is a little more mature, they may be able to cope with what follows.

- Break into groups of 3 or 4, and give them four possible understandings of the passage.

  - 1. The understanding given in *Getting Ready*.
  - 2. It's an example for us to follow in dealing with the world.
  - 3. It's a model of faithfulness to our Father in Heaven.
  - 4. It's an exhortation to be slightly selfish as we pursue our goal of following Jesus.

- Put these up on an OHP or poster on the wall.

- Ask your group to work out which is the correct understanding, and why. Make sure their answers are backed up with careful reference to the passage. After discussion together, make sure that everyone is clear about how this addresses positively a Christian's attitude to and use of possessions, both monetary and other.

FINAL WHISTLE

In the light of the Luke 16 passage, ask your group to consider how they can use what they own for God.

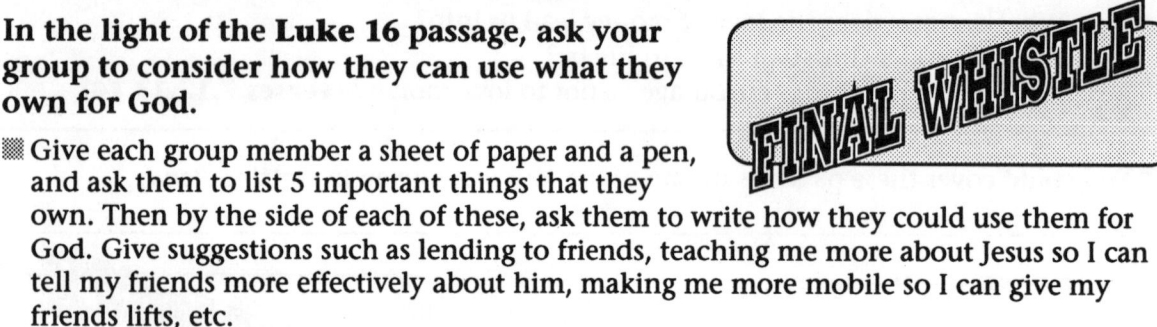

- Give each group member a sheet of paper and a pen, and ask them to list 5 important things that they own. Then by the side of each of these, ask them to write how they could use them for God. Give suggestions such as lending to friends, teaching me more about Jesus so I can tell my friends more effectively about him, making me more mobile so I can give my friends lifts, etc.

- Then ask them to write down something they would really like, and then write beside that how they would use it for God. Ask them if their possible use of it for God can justify them buying it, or whether they want it purely for their own use, enjoyment and partial satisfaction.

EXTRA TIME

Finally, try these:

- **1.** Conduct a brief and informal survey of the group's ownership of things like TV (how many?), VCR, walkman, trainers, CD, microwave, satellite, etc., and stress that there is in itself nothing wrong with owning any of these, or not owning any of them. But our attitude to them, or lack of them, is important.

- **2.** Play Monopoly, or at least a shortened version of the game.

- **3.** Write a brief case study of a Christian who is well off but tight-fisted, and wants to be even better off. Ask your group to write a postcard to them to teach them what the Bible has to say about this.

GROUP EXTRA

HOW I SPEND MY MONEY

50p	50p	50p	50p
£1	£1	£1	£1
20p	20p	20p	20p
20p	10p	10p	10p
10p	10p	10p	10p
10p	10p	10p	£5

EXPENDITURE PIE CHART

SESSION 10

Straight Talk – Homosexuality

Teaching Point

Homosexual activity is sinful. As with all sin, it should be avoided, but there is forgiveness in Christ for those who fail. Homosexual tendencies need to be controlled, as with any other desire to do what God has forbidden.

Group Action

Members to avoid any involvement in homosexual practices, whilst showing love and acceptance towards those whose inclinations are homosexual.

PRE-MATCH

Getting Ready

This is a delicate and controversial subject, which needs to be handled sensitively if young people are not be become even more confused than they may already be. Evidence suggests that a large proportion of people, especially boys, experience some degree of attraction to members of their own sex during adolescence. For the majority this is a 'phase' which does not last long, but for others it can persist long into adulthood. If young people become involved in homosexual activity during such a phase, they can be damaged for life.

There are only seven definite references to homosexuality in the Bible, and these are as follows:

Genesis 19 recalls the incident from which we derive the term 'sodomy', though it would be wrong to equate all homosexual activity with such an extreme episode. The subsequent destruction of the city by God is evidence of his judgement against its lifestyle.

Judges 19 is a strikingly similar story, except there is no divine intervention.

In both these accounts, the intended homosexual action was proposed by people who were equally prepared to indulge in heterosexual rape. It would be inappropriate to describe them as homosexuals. The clear intent was to abuse and degrade the intended victims rather than to fulfil a homosexual desire.

In **Leviticus 18:22** & **20:13** we are given clear statements outlawing homosexual sex in the strongest possible terms and treating it as an offence punishable by death.

Romans 1:18-27 is dealt with in detail in *First Half* as is **1 Corinthians 6:9-10.**

The final reference is **1 Timothy 1:9-10** which says much the same as in Corinthians. Paul is describing men who have homosexual intercourse. Whatever the motive or circumstance, it is the action which is a perversion, irrespective of how the participants might feel about it.

To summarise, whilst the Bible does not say a lot about homosexuality, what it does say is unequivocal and consistent – homosexual action is ALWAYS wrong.

Equipment

✓ Bibles, notebooks, pens, *Group Extra* sheets
✓ OHP/screen or posters/roll of paper
✓ OHP pens/acetate or marker pens
✓ Magazine or Video clips of media personalities

Music

I Am A New Creation
I Am Accepted, I Am Forgiven

Team Talk

Whilst homosexual acts are condemned in the Bible, nothing is explicitly said about homosexual feelings. This is an area of much controversy, even amongst Christians. Those who experience strong attraction towards others of the same sex often argue that this is the way God has made them and they cannot help their nature. Others see homosexual attraction as an illness to be cured.

The fact that the Bible makes no reference to the homosexual *nature* suggests that it is wrong to single out an inclination towards homosexual sin as deserving of special attention. What the Bible does teach is that we all share in common a human nature, which is sinful.

How the sin principle at work within our human nature finds expression varies from person to person. One person may have a tendency to steal, another to lie and so on. We all have a tendency to sin, but we don't all have a tendency to commit the same sins. The sins we commit can be affected by a whole range of factors, including our upbringing and environment, some of which can build into our lives a pattern of behaviour which is very hard to change. But if we believe the gospel then change is possible. **Romans 6-8** deals thoroughly with this whole area.

Nevertheless, it may be that there is a need for special help and counselling for people who experience particular problems with regard to homosexual feelings. Addresses of organisations offering such help are given on page 64.

First Half looks at the passages outlined in *Getting Ready*. You will need to select from these passages as you feel appropriate, though suggestions are given.

Second Half will examine the teaching about homosexual sin in the context of sin in general.

WARM UP

Display a series of magazine pictures or brief video extracts of personalities whose images may be associated, however loosely, with homosexuality.

- These should range from female impersonators or 'drag' artists like Danny La Rue, through the 'camp' comedy performers such as Guy Siner ('Gruber' in 'Allo, 'Allo) and the more recent and deliberately 'outrageous' Julian Clary, to those known to have been involved in homosexual or lesbian relationships, e.g. Freddy Mercury and Martina Navratilova. Avoid anything which explicitly portrays homosexual activity.

- Follow up with a list of words on a large piece of paper or O.H.P. acetate, some deliberately emotive, suggesting reactions to these images. The list might include: funny, harmless, queer, sick, normal, perverted, effeminate, straight, gay, brave, sad.

- Ask the group to look at the list in silence for two or three minutes and try to formulate in their own minds, which words they would associate with the various personalities they have seen. They may wish to choose words which do not appear on your list. Stress that they will not be asked to disclose their thoughts.

KICK OFF

Without asking the group to actually say what words they linked to particular pictures, explain that it is likely that they will have experienced a range of feelings from 'funny' or 'harmless' through to 'sick' or 'perverted'. Some may have had positive reactions to people involved in long-term homosexual relationships as being 'brave' to admit to such relationships in the face of social pressures.

- Explain that our reactions will vary from image to image and from person to person. This may depend on our background, the attitudes of those around us and society in general, and possibly on our own feelings.

- Stress the importance of distinguishing between popular images of homosexuality, which may vary from complete acceptance to extremes of 'queer bashing', and what the Bible teaches.

FIRST HALF

Divide members into small groups to find out what the Bible has to teach.

- Begin with **Romans 1:18-27**. Pose the following questions and record answers on acetate or paper and display on a OHP/poster:

    1) What is the effect of wickedness?
       Suppresses truth. (V.18)

    2) Why do people have no excuse for not knowing God?
       He has revealed himself through creation. (V.19-20)

    3) What effect does rejecting God have?
       Thinking becomes futile; hearts are darkened. (V.21)

    4) What have people chosen to worship instead of their Creator?
       Mortal man, birds, animals, reptiles – created things. (V.22-23 & 25)

    5) What has God given them over to as a result?
       Sinful desires/shameful lusts. (V.24 & 26a)

6) How do these sinful desires find expression?
In sexual immorality (amongst other things), one aspect of which is homosexuality (both male and female). (V.24 & 26-27)

▓ Conclusion: Homosexual practice is a distortion of sexuality as God intended, brought about by our fallen, sinful nature. The clear inference is that when we lose sight of God as Creator, we lose our right perspective on His created order. This opens the door for all manner of distortions, one of which is the distortion of sexuality as God intended it to be. It is because our sexuality is so fundamental to our whole being and the continuance of the human race that Paul chooses this as the prime example of the distorrtion caused by sin.

▓ This is the only passage which refers to both 'lesbianism', or female homosexuality, and male homosexuality, and both are condemned. It is also significant that Paul says that those who indulge in homosexual acts will receive 'in themselves the due penalty for their perversion'. This suggests that such practices are self-destrctive.

▓ Get the group to read **Leviticus 18:22 & 20:13; 1 Corinthians 6:9-10**.

▓ The Corinthian passage lists a number of people who are 'wicked' and , therefore, will not inherit the kingdom of God. Amongst them are included 'male prostitutes' and 'homosexual offenders' (N.I.V.), translated in the Good News Bible together under the one description 'homosexual perverts'.

▓ Using the word 'pervert' is not the most helpful term and may allow for an incomplete understanding of what Paul says. This hinges on the distinction between 'perversion' and 'inversion'. The former description refers to people who are by nature hetrosexual indulging in homosexuality. The Genesis and Judges incidents would be examples of this.

▓ 'Inversion', however, refers to people who would consider themselves to be by nature homosexual and for whom heterosexual acts would be felt 'unnatural'.

▓ The Greek words Paul uses are *malakoi* and *arsenokoitai*. The former means effeminate and refers to aman taking the role of a woman in a sexual relationship. The latter is the 'male' or 'wooing' partner in such a relationship. The translation of these words by use of 'prostitute', 'offender' and 'pervert' may imply only homosexual acts for financial gain, as an illegal act, against the will of the partner or contrary to one's nature. Pau's usage is more general. He refers to any practice of homosexual intercourse whatever the relationship between the partners.

▓ Now answer the following questions using the passages from Leviticus and 1 Corinthians:

1) How does God describe homosexual activity? **Detestable.**

2) What punishment is given in the Old Testament? **Death.**

3) What punishment is given in the New Testament? **Exclusion from God's kingdom.**

▓ Record answers on acetate/paper.

▓ N.B. Homosexual practice has eternal consequences, because it represents a rejection of God's ways.

Each person should be given a copy of the *Group Extra* sheet, 'I AM...I DO...'.

▓ In the 'I AM..' column, they should circle the characteristics which they feel best describe themselves, choosing as far as possible one from each pair of opposites. On the 'I DO..' side there is a range of choice from 'ALWAYS' through to 'NEVER'. They should put a tick in the column which they think is nearest to the way they act. They should put a tick on every row, not just the one that relates most obviously to the characteristics they have circled.

- This exercise should show that whatever we feel our characteristics to be, whether good or bad, we don't *always* act in line with them. We may have occasional lapses in our good areas and sometimes overcome our weaknesses.

- What should we, therefore, conclude about homosexual feelings? If God clearly teaches in his word that homosexual activity is wrong, then we cannot accept that it is inevitable that homosexual feelings should lead to such activity. Like a bad temper, they can and should be brought under control. In this, we need the help of the Holy Spirit.

In this section we will look again at some of the Bible passages covered in *First Half* to see the context in which homosexuality is referred to.

SECOND HALF

- Using a large sheet of paper or OHP acetate, mark out three columns headed: SIN, VERDICT, and SENTENCE. Get the group to list some of the different types of sin mentioned in **Leviticus 18 & 20**, God's verdict on them and the sentence passed.

- Now point out the following:

Leviticus 18:22

- This verse is just one of God's rules about His intention for people in the expression of their sexuality. Homosexual acts are wrong but so are all the other sexual acts described. It would be wrong to single out homosexuality for particular condemnation.

Leviticus 20:13

- In this case we find God's sanction against homosexual activity and there is no mistaking the severity of the punishment, which reflects the seriousness of the act. However, we should again see that it is set in the context of God's sanctions against other sins, most but not all of which involve sexual acts and many of which attract the same penalty.

- Now repeat the exercise, using **Romans 1:24-32**.

- Having already looked at **V 18-27**, this time pick up the passage at **V 24** but carry on through to the end of the chapter.

The above exercise should show us the seriousness of homosexual sin but also the seriousness of ALL sin.

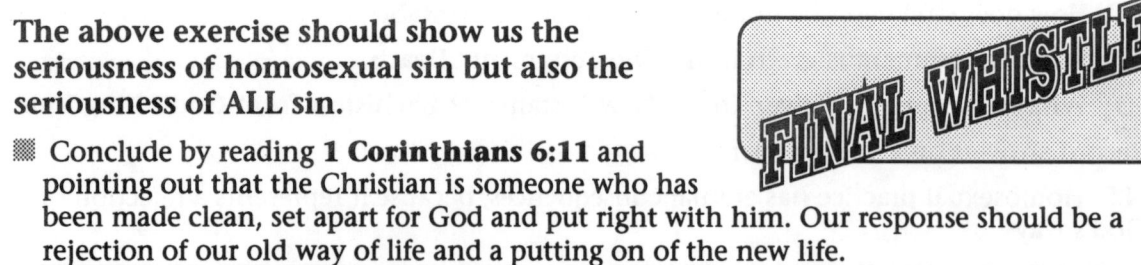

FINAL WHISTLE

- Conclude by reading **1 Corinthians 6:11** and pointing out that the Christian is someone who has been made clean, set apart for God and put right with him. Our response should be a rejection of our old way of life and a putting on of the new life.

- We have no right to condemn others because of a particular sin. We all need God's forgiveness and continuing strength if we are to live the way He intends us to.

- **1)** Whilst not dealing with the particular issue of homosexuality, it is worth looking at **John 8:1-11** and how Jesus condemned the sin but not the sinner.

EXTRA TIME

- **2)** Ask the group to sit with their eyes closed and imagine a person wrestling with homosexual feelings. Read aloud **Romans 7:15-8:17**.

GROUP EXTRA

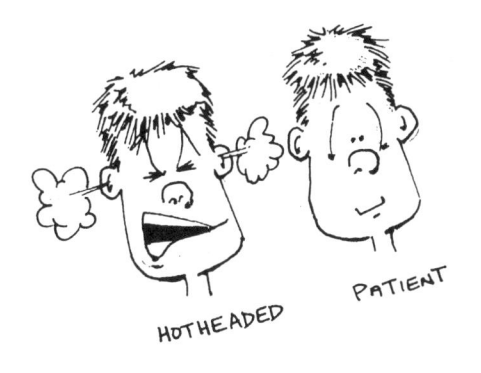

'I AM...'		'I DO...'			
			ALWAYS	OFTEN	SOMETIMES	NEVER
Hotheaded	Patient	Lose my temper				
		Stay cool				
Shy	Extrovert	Keep quiet				
		Talk a lot				
Liar	Honest	Tell lies				
		Tell the truth				
Dependable	Unreliable	Keep my word				
		Let people down				
Lazy	Hard working	Avoid work				
		Stick at it				
Cheerful	Miserable	Smile				
		Sulk				

Some Useful Addresses

Inclusion of an address does not neccessarily imply endorsement of the beliefs and policies of the organisation. Not all are Christian and some which come under the Christian banner may not be orthodox evangelical. Some organisations publish newsletters, magazines or may provide visiting speakers. List correct as at December 1992.

A.C.E.T. (Aids Care Education and Training)
P.O.Box 1323, LONDON W5 5TF.
Tel. 081 840 7879 — Section 4

Alcoholics Anonymous
P.O.Box 1, Stonebow House, Stonebow,
YORK Y01 2NJ. Tel. 0904 644026 — Section 1

Christian Action
St, Peter's House, 308 Kennington Lane,
LONDON SE11 5HY.
Tel. 071 735 2372 — Section 6

Christian Aid
P.O.Box 100, LONDON SE1 7RT.
Tel. 071 620 4444 — Section 7

Christian Broadcasting Campaign
91 Hallam Way, West Hallam,
DERBY DE7 6LD. Tel. 0602 307552 — Section 8

Christians For Social Justice
31 Prince of Wales Lane, Yardley Wood,
BIRMINGHAM, West Midlands B14 4LB.
Tel: 021 430 8980 — Section 2

Christian Impact
St. Peter's Church, Vere Street,
LONDON W1M 9HP. Tel. 071 629 3615 — General

Christian initiative on Teenage Sexuality
(Extensive database of resources on all aspects of sex and sexuality) 46 Green Road, Hall Green,
BIRMINGHAM B28 8DD.
Tel. 021 777 8957 — Section 4,10

Church Action on Poverty
Central Buildings, Oldham Street, MANCHESTER M11JT. Tel. 061 236 9321 — Section 2

Commission for Racial Equality
Elliot House, 10/12 Allington Street,
LONDON SW1E 5EH. — Section 6

Courage
P.O.Box 338, WATFORD, Hertfordshire
WD1 4BQ. Tel. 0923 247017 — Section 10

Crises Centre Ministries
12 City Road, St. Paul's,
BRISTOL BS2 8TP. Tel. 0272 423088 — Section 1

Equal Opportunities Commission (H.Q.)
Overseas House, Quay Street, MANCHESTER
M3 3HN. Tel. 061 833 9244 — Section 6

Evangelical Christians for Racial Justice
12 Bell Barn Shopping Centre,
Cregoe Street, BIRMINGHAM B15 2DZ.
Tel. 021 622 5799 — Section 6

Fellowship of Faith for Muslims
P.O.Box 58, WAKEFIELD, West Yorkshire
WF2 9AN. Tel. 0924 386513 — Section 5

Friends of the Earth
26 Underwood Street, LONDON N1 7JQ.
Tel. 071 490 1555 — Section 3

Greenpeace
30 Islington Green, London N1 8XE.
Tel. 071 354 5100 — Section 3

Health Education Authority
Hamilton House, Mabledon Place, LONDON
WC1H 9TX. Tel. 071 383 3833 — Section 1,4

Kalaidoscope Project
40 Cromwell Road, KINGSTON-UPON-THAMES,
Surrey KT2 6RE. Tel. 081 549 2681 — Section 1, 2

Mildmay Mission Hospital
Hackney Road, Shoreditch, LONDON E2 7NA.
Tel. 071 739 2331 — Section 4

National Viewers and Listeners Association
Ardleigh, COLCHESTER, Essex CO7 7RH.
Tel. 0206 230123 — Section 8

Oasis Trust
Haddon Hall, 22 Tower Bridge Road, LONDON
SE1 4TR. Tel. 071 231 4637 — Section 2

Oxfam
274 Banbury Road, OXFORD OX2 7DZ.
Tel. 0865 311311 — Section 7

Pilot Trust
Shankhill Road Mission, 116 Shankhill Road,
BELFAST BT13 2BD.
Tel. 0232 230743 — Section 10

Reachout Trust
(Mission to those involved in occult, New Age, cults.) Alpha Place, Garth Road, MORDEN,
Surrey SM4 4LX. Tel. 081 337 9716 — Section 5

Scottish Band of Hope
23 Royal Exchange Square,
GLASGOW G1 3AJ. Tel. 041 221 5077 — Section 1

Shelter
88 Old Street, LONDON EC1V 9HU.
Tel. 071 253 0202 — Section 2

Simon Community
129 Malden Road, LONDON NW5 4HW.
Tel. 071 485 6639 — Section 2

Tear Fund
100 Church Road, TEDDINGTON, Middlesex
TW11 8QE. Tel. 081 977 9144 — Section 2, 7, 9

True Freedom Trust
P.O.Box 3, Upton, WIRRAL, Merseyside L46 6NY.
Tel. 051 653 0773 — Section 10
also at: P.O. Box 592,
LONDON SE4 1EF. Tel. 081 314 5735

U.K. Band of Hope
25f Copperfield Street, LONDON SE1 0EN.
Tel. 071 928 0848 — Section 1

U-Turn Anglia Trust
P.O.Box 138, IPSWICH, Suffolk 1P4 4RY.
Tel. 0473 716121 — Section 10

World Vision
Department C092, Dychurch House,
8 Abington Street, NORTHAMPTON NN1 2AJ.
Tel. 0604 22964 — Section 7, 9

Zebra Project
Bow Mission, 1 Merchant Street,
LONDON E3 4LY. — Section 6